THE ESSENE GOSPEL OF PEACE

Books 1-4

The Third Century Aramaic Manuscript and old Slavonic Texts
Compared, Edited, and Translated by

Edmond Bordeaux Szekely

Book One: The Essene Gospel of Peace
Book Two: The Unknown Books of the Essenes
Book Three: Lost Scrolls of the Essene Brotherhood
Book Four: The Teachings of the Elect

Published by AudioEnlightenment.com

Copyright © 2018 by AudioEnlightenment, All rights reserved. No part of this publication may be reproduced, distributed, or transmitted in any form or by any means, including photocopying, recording, or other electronic or mechanical methods, without the prior written permission of the publisher, except in the case of brief quotations embodied in critical reviews and certain other noncommercial uses permitted by copyright law.

Printed in the United States of America

0 1 2 3 4 5 6 7 8 9

First Printing, 2018

ISBN 978-1-941489-40-6

www.MetaphysicalPocketBooks.Com

www.AudioEnlightenment.Com

Available on iTunes / Audible as Audio Book

First AudioEnlightenment Printing

April 2018

The spirits of truth and falsehood.

Struggle within the heart of man;

Truth born out of the spring of Light,

Falsehood from the well of darkness.

And according as a man inherits truth

So will he avoid darkness.

From the Manual of Discipline
of the Dead Sea Scrolls

Forward

Nearly 2000 years have passed since the Son of Man taught the way, the truth, and the life to mankind. He brought health to the sick, wisdom to the ignorant, and happiness to those in misery.

His words became half-forgotten and were not collected till some generations after they were uttered. They have been misunderstood, wrongly annotated, hundreds of times rewritten, and hundreds of times transformed, yet they have nevertheless survived almost 2000 years.

And though his words, as we have them today in the New Testament, have been terribly mutilated and deformed, they nevertheless have conquered half of humanity and the whole of the civilization of the West. This fact proves the eternal vitality of the Master's words, and their supreme and incomparable value.

The content of this book represents only about a third of the complete manuscripts which exist in Aramaic in the archives of the Vatican, and in old Slavonic in the Royal Archives of the Habsburgs, now the property of the Austrian government.

We owe the existence of these two versions to the Nestorian priests who, under pressure of the advancing hordes of Genghis Khan, were forced to flee from the East towards the West, bearing all their ancient scriptures and icons with them.

The ancient Aramaic texts date from the third century after Christ, while the old Slavonic version is a literal translation of the former. Exactly how these texts traveled from Palestine to the interior of Asia, into the hands of the Nestorian priests, archaeology is not yet able to reconstruct for us.

We have nothing to add to this text. It speaks for itself. The reader who studies the pages that follow with concentration will feel the eternal vitality and powerful evidence of these profound truths which mankind needs today more urgently than ever before.

"And the truth shall bear witness of itself."

London, 1937   Edmond Bordeaux Szekely

They sent out healers. And one of these was Jesus, the Essene. He walked among the sick and the troubled, and he brought them the knowledge they needed to cure themselves. Some who followed him wrote down what passed between him and those who suffered and were heavy-laden. The elders of the brotherhood made poetry of the words and made unforgettable the story of the Healer of Men, the Good Shepherd. And when the time came at last for the Brothers to leave the desert and go to another place, the scrolls stayed behind, as buried sentinels, as forgotten guardians of eternal and living truth.

A dark age began, a time of savagery, of barbarism, of book burning, of superstition and worship of empty idols. The gentle Jesus was lost forever in the image of a crucified God; the Essene brothers hid their teachings in the minds of a few who could preserve them for their descendants, and the scrolls of healing lay neglected beneath the shifting shadows of the desert.

The Discovery of the Essene Gospel of Peace
by Edmond Bordeaux Szekely

Contents

Book One: The Essene Gospel of Peace...........................1

Book Two: The Unknown Books of the Essenes................ 43

Book Three: Lost Scrolls of The Essene Brotherhood..........139

Book Four: The Teachings of the Elect........................... 253

THE ESSENE GOSPEL OF PEACE
Book One

THE ESSENE GOSPEL OF PEACE

And then many sick and maimed came to Jesus, asking him: "If you know all things, tell us, why do we suffer with these grievous plagues? Why are we not whole like other men? Master, heal us, that we too may be made strong, and need abide no longer in our misery. We know that you have it in your power to heal all manner of disease. Free us from Satan and from all his great afflictions. Master, have compassion on us."

And Jesus answered: "Happy are you, that you hunger for the truth, for I will satisfy you with the bread of wisdom. Happy are you, that you knock, for I will open to you the door of life. Happy are you, that you would cast off the power of Satan, for I will lead you into the kingdom of our Mother's angels, where the power of Satan cannot enter."

And they asked him in amazement: "Who is our Mother and which her angels? And where is her kingdom?"

"Your Mother is in you, and you in her. She bore you: she gives you life. It was she who gave to you your body, and to her shall you one day give it back again. Happy are you when you come to know her and her kingdom; if you receive your Mother's angels and if you do her laws. I tell you truly, he who does these things shall never see disease. For the power of our Mother is above all. And it destroys Satan and his kingdom and has rule over all your bodies and all living things.

"The blood which runs in us is born of the blood of our Earthly Mother. Her blood falls from the clouds; leaps up from the womb of the earth; babbles in the brooks of the mountains; flows wide in the rivers of the plains; sleeps in the lakes; rages mightily in tempestuous seas.

"The air which we breathe is born of the breath of our Earthly Mother. Her breath is azure in the heights of the heavens; soughs in the tops of the mountains; whispers in the leaves of the forest; billows over the cornfields; slumbers in the deep valleys; burns hot in the desert.

"The hardness of our bones is born of the bones of our Earthly Mother, of the rocks and of the stones. They stand naked to the heavens on the tops of the mountains; are as giants that lie sleeping on the sides of the mountains, as idols set in the desert, and are hidden in the deepness of the earth.

"The tenderness of our flesh is born of the flesh of our Earthly Mother, whose flesh waxes yellow and red in the fruits of the trees, and nurtures us in the furrows of the fields.

"Our bowels are born of the bowels of our Earthly Mother, and are hid from our eyes, like the invisible depths of the earth.

"The light of our eyes, the hearing of our ears, both are born of the colors and the sounds of our Earthly Mother which enclose us about, as the waves of the sea, a fish; as the eddying air, a bird.

"I tell you in very truth, Man is the Son of the Earthly Mother, and from her did the Son of Man receive his whole body, even as the body of the newborn babe is born of the womb of his mother. I tell you truly, you are one with the Earthly Mother; she is in you, and you in her. Of her were you born, in her do you live, and to her shall you return again. Keep, therefore, her laws, for none can live long, neither be happy, but he who honors his Earthly Mother and does her laws. For your breath is her breath; your blood her blood; your bone her bone; your flesh her flesh; your bowels her bowels; your eyes and your ears are her eyes and her ears.

"I tell you truly, should you fail to keep but one only of all these laws, should you harm but one only of all your body's members, you shall be utterly lost in your grievous sickness, and there shall be weeping and gnashing of teeth. I tell you, unless you follow the laws of your Mother, you can in no wise escape death. And he who clings to the laws of his Mother, to him shall his Mother cling also. She shall heal all his plagues, and he shall never become sick. She gives him long life, and protects him from all afflictions; from fire, from water, from the bite of venomous serpents. For your Mother bore you, keeps life within you. She has given you her body, and none but she heals you. Happy is he who loves his Mother and lies quietly in her bosom. For your Mother loves you, even when you turn away from her. And how much more shall she love you, if you turn to her again? I tell you truly, very great is her love, greater than the greatest of mountains, deeper than the deepest seas. And those who love their Mother, she never deserts them. As the hen protects her chickens, as the lioness her cubs, as the mother her newborn babe, so does the Earthly Mother protect the Son of Man from all danger and from all evils.

"For I tell you truly, evils and dangers innumerable lie in wait for the Sons of Men. Beelzebub, the prince of all devils, the source of every evil, lies in wait in the body of all the Sons of Men. He is death, the lord of every plague, and taking upon him a pleasing raiment, he tempts and entices the Sons of Men. Riches does he promise, and power, and splendid palaces, and garments of gold and silver, and a multitude of servants, all these; he promises renown and glory, fornication and lustfulness, gluttony and wine-bibbing, riotous living, and slothfulness and idle days. And he entices everyone by that to which their heart is most inclined. And in the day that the Sons of Men have already become the slaves of all these vanities and abominations, then in payment thereof he snatches from the Sons of Men all those things which the Earthly Mother gave them so abundantly. He takes from them their breath, their blood, their bone, their flesh, their bowels, their eyes and their ears. And the breath of the Son of Man becomes short and stifled, full of pain and evil-smelling, like the breath of unclean beasts. And his blood becomes thick and evil-smelling, like the water of the swamps; it clots and blackens, like the night of death. And his bone becomes hard and knotted; it melts away within and breaks asunder, as a stone falling down upon a rock. And his flesh waxes fat and watery; it rots and putrefies, with scabs and boils that are an abomination. And his bowels become full with abominable filthiness, with oozing streams of decay; and multitudes of abominable worms have their habitation there. And his eyes grow dim, till dark night enshrouds them, and his ears become stopped, like the silence of the grave. And last of all shall the erring Son of Man lose life. For he kept not the laws of his Mother, and added sin to sin. Therefore, are taken from him all the gifts of the Earthly Mother: breath, blood, bone, flesh, bowels, eyes and ears, and after all else, life, with which the Earthly Mother crowned his body.

"But if the erring Son of Man be sorry for his sins and undo them, and return again to his Earthly Mother; and if he do his Earthly Mother's laws and free himself from Satan's clutches, resisting his temptations, then does the Earthly Mother receive again her erring Son with love and sends him her angels that they may serve him. I tell you truly, when the Son of Man resists the Satan that dwells in him and does not his will, in the same hour are found the Mother's angels there, that they may serve him with all their power and free utterly the Son of Man from the power of Satan.

"For no man can serve two masters. For either he serves Beelzebub and his devils or else he serves our Earthly Mother and her angels. Either he serves death or he serves life. I tell you truly, happy are those that do the laws of life and wander not upon the paths of death. For in them the forces of life wax strong and they escape the plagues of death."

And all those round about him listened to his words with amazement, for his word was with power, and he taught quite otherwise than the priests and scribes.

And though the sun was now set, they departed not to their homes. They sat round about Jesus and asked him: "Master, which are these laws of life? Rest with us awhile longer and teach us. We would listen to your teaching that we may be healed and become righteous."

And Jesus himself sat down in their midst and said: "I tell you truly, none can be happy, except he do the Law."

And the others answered: "We all do the laws of Moses, our lawgiver, even as they are written in the holy scriptures."

And Jesus answered: "Seek not the Law in your scriptures, for the Law is life, whereas the scripture is dead. I tell you truly, Moses received not his laws from God in writing, but through the living word. The Law is living word of living God to living prophets for living men. In everything that is life is the Law written. You find it in the grass, in the tree, in the river, in the mountain, in the birds of heaven, in the fishes of the sea; but seek it chiefly in yourselves. For I tell you truly, all living things are nearer to God than the scripture which is without life. God so made life and all living things that they might by the everlasting word teach the laws of the true God to man. God wrote not the laws in the pages of books, but in your heart and in your spirit. They are in your breath, your blood, your bone; in your flesh, your bowels, your eyes, your ears, and in every little part of your body. They are present in the air, in the water, in the earth, in the plants, in the sunbeams, in the depths and in the heights. They all speak to you that you may understand the tongue and the will of the living God. But you shut your eyes that you may not see, and you shut your ears that you may not hear. I tell you truly, that the scripture is the work of man, but life and all its hosts are the work of our God. Wherefore do you not listen to the words of God which are written in His works? And wherefore do you study the dead scriptures which are the work of the hands of men?"

"How may we read the laws of God elsewhere than in the scriptures? Where are they written? Read them to us from there where you see them, for we know nothing else but the scriptures which we have inherited from our forefathers. Tell us the laws of which you speak, that hearing them we may be healed and justified."

Jesus said: "You do not understand the words of life, because you are in death. Darkness darkens your eyes and your ears are stopped with deafness. For I tell you, it profits you not at all that you pore over dead scriptures if by your deeds you deny him who has given you the scriptures. I tell you truly, God and his laws are not in that which you do. They are not in gluttony and in wine-bibbing, neither in riotous living, nor in lustfulness, nor in seeking after riches, nor yet in hatred of your enemies. For all these things are far from the true God and from his angels. But all these things come from the kingdom of darkness and the lord of all evils. And all these things do you carry in yourselves; and so the word and the power of God enter not into you, because all manner of evil and all manner of abominations have their dwelling in your body and your spirit. If you will that the living God's word and his power may enter you, defile not your body and your spirit; for the body is the temple of the spirit, and the spirit is the temple of God. Purify, therefore, the temple, that the Lord of the temple may dwell therein and occupy a place that is worthy of him.

"And from all temptations of your body and your spirit, coming from Satan, withdraw beneath the shadow of God's heaven.

"Renew yourselves and fast. For I tell you truly, that Satan and his plagues may only be cast out by fasting and by prayer. Go by yourself and fast alone, and show your fasting to no man. The living

God shall see it and great shall be your reward. And fast till Beelzebub and all his evils depart from you, and all the angels of our Earthly Mother come and serve you. For I tell you truly, except you fast, you shall never be freed from the power of Satan and from all diseases that come from Satan. Fast and pray fervently, seeking the power of the living God for your healing. While you fast, eschew the Sons of Men and seek our Earthly Mother's angels, for he that seeks shall find.

"Seek the fresh air of the forest and of the fields, and there in the midst of them shall you find the Angel of Air. Put off your shoes and your clothing and suffer the Angel of Air to embrace all your body. Then breathe long and deeply, that the Angel of Air may be brought within you. I tell you truly, the Angel of Air shall cast out of your body all uncleannesses which defiled it without and within. And thus shall all evil-smelling and unclean things rise out of you, as the smoke of fire curls upwards and is lost in the sea of the air. For I tell you truly, holy is the Angel of Air, who cleanses all that is unclean and makes all evil-smelling things of a sweet odor. No man may come before the face of God, whom the Angel of Air lets not pass. Truly, all must be born again by air and by truth, for your body breathes the air of the Earthly Mother, and your spirit breathes the truth of the Heavenly Father.

"After the Angel of Air, seek the Angel of Water. Put off your shoes and your clothing and suffer the Angel of Water to embrace all your body. Cast yourselves wholly into his enfolding arms, and as often as you move the air with your breath, move with your body the water also. I tell you truly, the Angel of Water shall cast out of your body all uncleannesses which defiled it without and within. And all unclean and evil-smelling things shall flow out of you, even as the uncleannesses of garments washed in water flow away and are lost in the stream of the river. I tell you truly, holy is the Angel of Water who cleanses all that is unclean and makes all evil-smelling things of a sweet odor. No man may come before the face of God whom the Angel of Water lets not pass. In very truth, all must be born again of water and of truth, for your body bathes in the river of life everlasting. For you receive your blood from our Earthly Mother and the truth from our Heavenly Father.

"Think not that it is sufficient that the Angel of Water embrace you outwards only. I tell you truly, the uncleanness within is greater by much than the uncleanness without. And he who cleanses himself without, but within remains unclean, is like to tombs that outwards are painted fair, but are within full of all manner of horrible uncleannesses and abominations. So I tell you truly, suffer the Angel of Water to baptize you also within, that you may become free from all your past sins, and that within likewise you may become as pure as the river's foam sporting in the sunlight.

"Seek, therefore, a large trailing gourd, having a stalk the length of a man; take out its inwards and fill it with water from the river which the sun has warmed. Hang it upon the branch of a tree, and kneel upon the ground before the Angel of Water, and suffer the end of the stalk of the trailing gourd to enter your hinder parts, that the water may flow through all your bowels. Afterwards, rest kneeling on the ground before the Angel of Water and pray to the living God that he will forgive you all your past sins, and pray the Angel of Water that he will free your body from every uncleanness and disease. Then let the water run out from your body, that it may carry away from within it all the unclean and evil-smelling things of Satan. And you shall see with your eyes and smell with your nose all the abominations, and uncleannesses which defiled the temple of your body; even all the sins which abode in your body, tormenting you with all manner of pains. I tell you truly, baptism with water frees you from all of these. Renew your baptizing with water on every day of your fast, till the day when you see that the water which flows out of you is as pure as the river's foam. Then betake your body to the coursing river, and there, in the arms of the Angel of Water, render thanks to the living God that he has freed you from your sins. And this holy baptizing by the Angel of Water is: Rebirth unto the new life. For your eyes shall henceforth see, and your ears shall hear. Sin no more, therefore, after your baptism, that the Angels of Air and of Water may eternally abide in you and serve you evermore.

"And if afterward there remain within you aught of your past sins and uncleannesses, seek the Angel of Sunlight. Put off your shoes and your clothing and suffer the Angel of Sunlight to embrace all your body. Then breathe long and deeply, that the Angel of Sunlight may be brought within you. And the Angel of Sunlight shall cast out of your body all evil-smelling and unclean things which defiled it without and within. And all unclean and evil-smelling things shall rise from you, even as the darkness of night fades before the brightness of the rising sun. For I tell you truly, holy is the Angel of Sunlight who cleans out all uncleannesses and makes all evil-smelling things of a sweet odor. None may come before the face of God, whom the Angel of Sunlight lets not pass. Truly, all must be born again of sun and of truth, for your body basks in the sunlight of the Earthly Mother, and your spirit basks in the sunlight of the truth of the Heavenly Father.

"The Angels of Air and of Water and of Sunlight are brethren. They were given to the Son of Man that they might serve him, and that he might go always from one to the other.

"Holy, likewise, is their embrace. They are indivisible children of the Earthly Mother, so do not you put asunder those whom earth and heaven have made one. Let these three brother angels enfold you every day and let them abide with you through all your fasting.

"For I tell you truly, the power of devils, all sins and uncleannesses shall depart in haste from that body which is embraced by these three angels. As thieves flee from a deserted house at the coming of the lord of the house, one by the door, one by the window, and the third by the roof, each where he is found, and whither he is able, even so shall flee from your bodies all devils of evil, all past sins, and all uncleannesses and diseases which defiled the temple of your bodies. When the Earthly Mother's angels enter into your bodies, in such wise that the lords of the temple repossess it again, then shall all evil smells depart in haste by your breath and by your skin, corrupt waters by your mouth and by your skin, by your hinder and your privy parts. And all these things you shall see with your eyes and smell with your nose and touch with your hands. And when all sins and uncleannesses are gone from your body, your blood shall become as pure as our Earthly Mother's blood and as the river's foam sporting in the sunlight. And your breath shall become as pure as the breath of odorous flowers; your flesh as pure as the flesh of fruits reddening upon the leaves of trees; the light of your eye as clear and bright as the brightness of the sun shining upon the blue sky. And now shall all the Angels of the Earthly Mother serve you. And your breath, your blood, your flesh shall be one with the breath, the blood and the flesh of the Earthly Mother, that your spirit also may become one with the spirit of your Heavenly Father. For truly, no one can reach the Heavenly Father unless through the Earthly Mother. Even as no newborn babe can understand the teaching of his father till his mother has suckled him, bathed him, nursed him, put him to sleep and nurtured him. While the child is yet small, his place is with his mother and he must obey his mother. When the child is grown up, his father takes him to work at his side in the field, and the child comes back to his mother only when the hour of dinner and supper is come. And now his father teaches him, that he may become skilled in the works of his father. And when the father sees that his son understands his teaching and does his work well, he gives him all his possessions, that they may belong to his beloved son, and that his son may continue his father's work. I tell you truly, happy is that son who accepts the counsel of his mother and walks therein. And a hundred times more happy is that son who accepts and walks also in the counsel of his father, for it was said to you: 'Honor thy father and thy mother that thy days may be long upon this earth.' But I say to you, Sons of Man: Honor your Earthly Mother and keep all her laws, that your days may be long on this earth, and honor your Heavenly Father that Eternal Life may be yours in the heavens. For the Heavenly Father is a hundred times greater than all fathers by seed and by blood, and greater is the Earthly Mother than all mothers by the body. And dearer is the Son of Man in the eyes of his Heavenly Father and of his Earthly Mother than are children in the eyes of their fathers by seed and by blood and of their mothers by the body. And more wise are the words and laws of your Heavenly Father and of your Earthly Mother than the words and the will of all fathers by seed and by blood, and of all mothers by the body. And of more worth also is the inheritance of your Heavenly Father and of your Earthly Mother, the everlasting kingdom of earthly and heavenly life, than all the inheritances of your fathers by seed and by blood, and of your mothers by the body.

"And your true brothers are all those who do the will of your Heavenly Father and of your Earthly Mother, and not your brothers by blood. I tell you truly, that your true brothers in the will of the Heavenly Father and of the Earthly Mother will love you a thousand times more than your brothers by blood. For since the days of Cain and Abel, when brothers by blood transgressed the will of God, there is no true brotherhood by blood. And brothers do unto brothers as do strangers. Therefore, I say to you, love your true brothers in the will of God a thousand times more than your brothers by blood.

FOR YOUR HEAVENLY FATHER IS LOVE.

FOR YOUR EARTHLY MOTHER IS LOVE.

FOR THE SON OF MAN IS LOVE.

"It is by love that the Heavenly Father and the Earthly Mother and the Son of Man become one. For the spirit of the Son of Man was created from the spirit of the Heavenly Father, and his body from the body of the Earthly Mother. Become, therefore, perfect as the spirit of your Heavenly Father and the body of your Earthly Mother are perfect. And so love your Heavenly Father, as he loves your spirit. And so love your Earthly Mother, as she loves your body. And so love your true brothers, as your Heavenly Father and your Earthly Mother love them. And then your Heavenly Father shall give you his holy spirit, and your Earthly Mother shall give you her holy body. And then shall the Sons of Men like true brothers give love one to another, the love which they received from their Heavenly Father and from their Earthly Mother; and they shall all become comforters one of another. And then shall disappear from the earth all evil and all sorrow, and there shall be love and joy upon earth. And then shall the earth be like the heavens, and the kingdom of God shall come. And then shall come the Son of Man in all his glory, to inherit the kingdom of God. And then shall the Sons of Men divide their divine inheritance, the kingdom of God. For the Sons of Men live in the Heavenly Father and in the Earthly Mother, and the Heavenly Father and the Earthly Mother live in them. And then with the kingdom of God shall come the end of the times. For the Heavenly Father's love gives to all life everlasting in the kingdom of God. For love is eternal. Love is stronger than death.

"Though I speak with the tongues of men and of angels, but have not love, I am sounding brass or a tinkling cymbal. Though I tell what is to come, and know all secrets, and all wisdom; and though I have faith strong as the storm which lifts mountains from their seat, but have not love, I am nothing. And though I bestow all my goods to feed the poor, and give all my fire that I have received from my Father, but have not love, I am in no wise profited. Love is patient, love is kind. Love is not envious, works not evil, knows not pride; is not rude, neither selfish; is slow to anger, imagines no mischief;

rejoices not in injustice, but delights in justice. Love defends all, love believes all, love hopes all, love bears all; never exhausts itself; but as for tongues they shall cease, and, as for knowledge, it shall vanish away. For we have truth in part, and error in part, but when the fullness of perfection is come, that which is in part shall be blotted out. When a man was a child he spoke as a child, understood as a child, thought as a child; but when he became a man he put away childish things. For now we see through a glass and through dark sayings. Now we know in part, but when we are come before the face of God, we shall not know in part, but even as we are taught by him. And now remain these three: faith and hope and love; but the greatest of these is love.

"And now I speak to you in the living tongue of the living God, through the holy spirit of our Heavenly Father. There is none yet among you that can understand all this of which I speak. He who expounds to you the scriptures speaks to you in a dead tongue of dead men, through his diseased and mortal body. Him, therefore, can all men understand, for all men are diseased and all are in death. No one sees the light of life. Blind man leads blind on the dark paths of sins, diseases and sufferings; and at the last, all fall into the pit of death.

"I am sent to you by the Father, that I may make the light of life to shine before you. The light lightens itself and the darkness, but the darkness knows only itself, and knows not the light. I have still many things to say to you, but you cannot bear them yet. For your eyes are used to the darkness, and the full light of the Heavenly Father would make you blind. Therefore, you cannot yet understand that which I speak to you concerning the Heavenly Father who sent me to you. Follow, therefore, first, only the laws of your Earthly Mother, of which I have told you. And when her angels shall have cleansed and renewed your bodies and strengthened your eyes, you will be able to bear the light of our Heavenly Father. When you can gaze on the brightness of the noonday sun with unflinching eyes, you can then look upon the blinding light of your Heavenly Father, which is a thousand times brighter than the brightness of a thousand suns. But how should you look upon the blinding light of your Heavenly Father, when you cannot even bear the shining of the blazing sun? Believe me, the sun is as the flame of a candle beside the sun of truth of the Heavenly Father. Have but faith, therefore, and hope, and love. I tell you truly, you shall not want your reward. If you believe in my words, you believe in him who sent me, who is the lord of all, and with whom all things are possible. For what is impossible with men, all these things are possible with God. If you believe in the Angels of the Earthly Mother and do her laws, your faith shall sustain you and you shall never see disease. Have hope also in the love of your Heavenly Father, for he who trusts in him shall never be deceived, nor shall he ever see death.

"Love one another, for God is love, and so shall his angels know that you walk in his paths. And then shall all the angels come before your face and serve you. And Satan with all sins, diseases, and uncleannesses shall depart from your body. Go, eschew your sins; repent yourselves; baptize yourselves; that you may be born again and sin no more."

Then Jesus rose. But all else remained sitting, for every man felt the power of his words. And then the full moon appeared between the breaking clouds and folded Jesus in its brightness. And sparks flew upward from his hair, and he stood among them in the moonlight, as though he hovered in the air. And no man moved, neither was the voice of any heard. And no one knew how long a time had passed, for time stood still.

Then Jesus stretched out his hands to them and said: "Peace be with you." And so he departed, as a breath of wind sways the green of trees.

And for a long while yet the company sat still and then they woke in the silence, one man after another, like as from a long dream. But none would go, as if the words of him who had left them ever sounded in their ears. And they sat as though they listened to some wondrous music.

But at last one, as it were a little fearfully, said: "How good it is to be here." Another: "Would that this night were everlasting." And others: "Would that he might be with us always." "Of a truth he is God's messenger, for he planted hope within our hearts." And no man wished to go home, saying: "I go not home where all is dark and joyless. Why should we go home where no one loves us?"

And they spoke on this wise, for they were almost all poor, lame, blind, maimed, beggars, homeless, despised in their wretchedness, who were only borne for pity's sake in the houses where they found a few days' refuge. Even certain, who had both home and family, said: "We also will stay with you." For every man felt that the words of him who was gone bound the little company with threads invisible. And all felt that they were born again. They saw before them a shining world, even when the moon was hidden in the clouds. And in the hearts of all blossomed wondrous flowers of wondrous beauty, the flowers of joy.

And when the bright sunbeams appeared over the earth's rim, they all felt that it was the sun of the coming kingdom of God. And with joyful countenances they went forth to meet God's angels.

And many unclean and sick followed Jesus' words and sought the banks of the murmuring streams. They put off their shoes and their clothing, they fasted, and they gave up their bodies to the Angels of Air, of Water, and of Sunshine. And the Earthly Mother's angels embraced them, possessing their bodies both inwards and outwards. And all of them saw all evils, sins, and uncleannesses depart in haste from them.

And the breath of some became as stinking as that which is loosed from the bowels, and some had an issue of spittle, and evil-smelling and unclean vomit rose from their inward parts. All these uncleannesses flowed by their mouths. In some, by the nose, in others by the eyes and ears. And many did have a noisome and abominable sweat come from all their body, over all their skin. And on many limbs great hot boils broke forth, from which came out uncleannesses with an evil smell, and urine flowed abundantly from their body; and in many their urine was all but dried up and became thick as the honey of bees; that of others was almost red or black, and as hard almost as the sand of rivers. And many belched stinking gases from their bowels, like the breath of devils. And their stench became so great that none could bear it.

And when they baptized themselves, the Angel of Water entered their bodies, and from them flowed out all the abominations and uncleannesses of their past sins, and like a falling mountain stream gushed from their bodies a multitude of hard and soft abominations. And the ground where their waters flowed was polluted, and so great became the stench that none could remain there. And the devils left their bowels in the shape of multitudinous worms which writhed in impotent rage after the Angel of Water had cast them out of the bowels of the Sons of Men. And then descended upon them the power of the Angel of Sunshine, and they perished there in their desperate writhings, trod underfoot by the Angel of Sunshine. And all were trembling with terror when they looked upon all these abominations of Satan, from which the angels had saved them. And they rendered thanks to God who had sent his angels for their deliverance.

And there were some whom great pains tormented, which would not depart from them; and knowing not what they should do, they resolved to send one of them to Jesus, for they greatly wished he should be with them.

And when two were gone to seek him, they saw Jesus himself approaching by the bank of the river. And their hearts were filled with hope and joy when they heard his greeting, "Peace be with you." And many were the questions that they desired to ask him, but in their astonishment they could not begin, for nothing came into their minds. Then said Jesus to them: "I come because you need me." And one cried out: "Master, we do indeed, come and free us from our pains."

And Jesus spoke to them in parables: "You are like the prodigal son, who for many years did eat and drink, and passed his days in riotousness and lechery with his friends. And every week without his father's knowledge he incurred new debts, and squandered all in a few days. And the moneylenders always lent to him, because his father possessed great riches and always paid patiently the debts of his son. And in vain did he with fair words admonish his son, for he never listened to the admonitions of his father, who besought him in vain that he would give up his debaucheries which had no end, and that he would go to his fields to watch over the labor of his servants. And the son always promised him everything if he would pay his old debts, but the next day he began again. And for more than seven years the son continued in his riotous living. But, at last, his father lost patience and no more paid to the moneylenders the debts of his son.

"If I continue always to pay," he said, "there will be no end to the sins of my son." Then the moneylenders, who were deceived, in their wrath took the son into slavery that he might by his daily toil pay back to them the money which he had borrowed. And then ceased the eating and drinking and the daily excesses. From morning until night by the sweat of his face he watered the fields, and all of his limbs ached with the unaccustomed labor. And he lived upon dry bread and had naught but his tears with which he could water it. And three days after he suffered so much from the heat and from weariness that he said to his master: 'I can work no more, for all my limbs do ache. How long would you torment me?' 'Till the day when by the labor of your hands you pay me all your debts, and when seven years are passed, you will be free.' And the desperate son answered, weeping: 'But I cannot bear so much as seven days. Have pity on me, for all my limbs do burn and ache.' And the wicked creditor cried out: 'Press on with the work; if you could for seven years spend your days and your nights in riotousness, now must you work for seven years. I will not forgive you till you pay back all your debts to the uttermost drachma.' And the son, with his limbs racked with pain, went back despairing to the fields to continue his work. Already he could hardly stand upon his feet because of his weariness and of his pains, when the seventh day was come—the Sabbath day, in which no man works in the field. Then the son gathered the remnant of his strength and staggered to the house of his father. And he cast himself down at his father's feet and said: 'Father, believe me for the last time and forgive me all my offenses against you. I swear to you that I will never again live riotously and that I will be your obedient son in all things. Free me from the hands of my oppressor. Father, look upon me and upon my sick limbs, and harden not your heart.' Then tears came into his father's eyes, and he took his son in his arms, and said: 'Let us rejoice, for today a great joy is given me, because I have found again my beloved son, who was lost.' And he clothed him with his choicest raiment and all the day long they made merry. And on the morning of the morrow he gave his son a bag of silver that he might pay to his creditors all that he owed them. And when his son came back, he said to him: 'My son, do you see that it is easy, through riotous living, to incur debts for seven years, but their payment is difficult by the heavy labor of seven years.' 'Father, it is indeed hard to pay them, even for seven days.' And his father admonished him, saying: 'For this once alone has it been permitted you to pay your debts in seven days instead of seven years; the rest is forgiven you. But take heed that in the time to come you do not incur more debts. For I tell you truly, that none else but your father forgives you your debts, because you are his son. For with all else you would have had to labor hard for seven years, as it is commanded in our laws.'

"'My father, I will henceforth be your loving and obedient son, and I will not any more incur debts, for I know that their payment is hard.'

"And he went to his father's field and watched every day over the work of his father's laborers. And he never made his laborers work hard, for he remembered his own heavy labor. And the years passed, and his father's possession increased ever more and more beneath his hand, for the blessing of his father was upon his labor. And slowly he gave back tenfold to his father all that he had squandered in the seven years. And when his father saw that his son used well his servants and all his possessions, he said to him: 'My son, I see that my possessions are in good hands. I give you all my cattle, my house, my lands and my treasures. Let all this be your heritage, continue increasing it that I may have delight in you.' And when the son had received his inheritance from his father, he forgave their debts to all his debtors who could not pay him, for he did not forget that his debt also had been forgiven when he could not pay it. And God blessed him with long life, with many children and with much riches, because he was kind to all his servants and to all his cattle."

Then Jesus turned to the sick folk and said: "I speak to you in parables that you may better understand God's word. The seven years of eating and drinking and of riotous living are the sins of the past. The wicked creditor is Satan. The debts are diseases. The heavy labor is pains. The prodigal son, he is yourselves. The payment of the debts is the casting from you of devils and diseases, and the healing of your body. The bag of silver received from the father is the liberating power of the angels. The father is God. The father's possessions are earth and heaven. The servants of the father are the Angels. The father's field is the world, which is changed into the kingdom of the heavens, if the Sons of Man work thereon together with the Angels of the Heavenly Father. For I tell you, it is better that the son should obey his father and keep watch over his father's servants in the field, than that he should become the debtor of the wicked creditor and toil and sweat in serfdom to repay all his debts. It is better, likewise, if the Sons of Man also obey the laws of their Heavenly Father, and work together with his angels upon his kingdom, than that they should become the debtors of Satan, the lord of death, of all sins and all diseases, and that they should suffer with pains and sweat till they have repaid all their sins. I tell you truly, great and many are your sins. Many years have you yielded to the enticings of Satan. You have been gluttonous, wine-bibbers, and gone a-whoring, and your past debts have multiplied. And now you must repay them, and payment is difficult and hard. Be not, therefore, already impatient after the third day, like the prodigal son, but wait patiently for the seventh day which is sanctified by God, and then go with humble and obedient heart before the face of your Heavenly Father, that he may forgive you your sins and all your past debts. I tell you truly, your Heavenly Father loves you without end, for he also allows you to pay in seven days the debts of seven years. Those that owe the sins and diseases of seven years, but pay honestly and persevere till the seventh day, to them shall our Heavenly Father forgive the debts of all these seven years.

"If we sin for seven times seven years?" asked a sick man who suffered horribly.

"Even in that case the Heavenly Father forgives you all your debts in seven times seven days."

"Happy are those that persevere to the end, for the devils of Satan write all your evil deeds in a book, in the book of your body and your spirit. I tell you truly, there is not one sinful deed, but it is written, even from the beginning of the world, before our Heavenly Father. For you may escape the laws made by kings, but the laws of your God, these may none of the Sons of Man escape. And when you come before the face of God, the devils of Satan bear witness against you with your deed, and God sees your sins written in the book of your body and of your spirit and is sad in his heart. But if you repent of your sins, and by fasting and prayer you seek the Angels of God, then each day that you continue to fast and to pray, God's angels blot out one year of your evil deeds from the book of your body and your spirit. And when the last page is also blotted out and cleansed from all your sins, you stand before the face of God, and God rejoices in his heart and forgets all your sins. He frees you from the clutches of Satan and from suffering; he takes you within his house and commands that all his servants, all his angels, serve you. Long life does he give you, and you shall never see disease. And if, thenceforward, instead of sinning, you pass your days in doing good deeds, then the Angels of God shall write all your good deeds in the book of your body and of your spirit. I tell you truly, no good deed remains unwritten before God, not from the beginning of the world. For from your kings and your governors you may wait in vain for your reward, but never do your good deeds want their reward from God.

"And when you come before the face of God, his angels bear witness for you with your good deeds. And God sees your good deeds written in your bodies and in your spirits, and rejoices in his heart. He blesses your body and your spirit and all your deeds, and gives you for a heritage his earthly and heavenly kingdom, that in it you may have life everlasting. Happy is he who can enter into the kingdom of God, for he shall never see death."

And a great silence fell at his words. And those that were discouraged took new strength from his words and continued to fast and to pray. And he who had spoken the first, said to him: "I will persevere to the seventh day." And the second, likewise, said to him: "I also will persevere to the seven times seventh day."

Jesus answered them: "Happy are those that persevere to the end, for they shall inherit the earth."

And there were many sick among them, tormented with grievous pains, and they hardly crawled to Jesus' feet. For they could no longer walk upon their feet. They said: "Master, we are grievously tormented with pain; tell us what we shall do." And they showed Jesus their feet in which the bones were twisted and knotted and said: "Neither the Angel of Air, nor of Water, nor of Sunshine has assuaged our pains, notwithstanding that we baptized ourselves, and do fast and pray, and follow your words in all things."

"I tell you truly, your bones will be healed. Be not discouraged, but seek for cure nigh the healer of bones, the Angel of Earth. For thence were your bones taken, and thither will they return."

And he pointed with his hand to where the running of the water and the sun's heat had softened to clayey mud the earth by the edge of the water. "Sink your feet in the mire, that the embrace of the Angel of Earth may draw out from your bones all uncleanness and all disease. And you will see Satan and your pains fly from the embrace of the Angel of Earth. And the knots of your bones will vanish away, and they will be straightened, and all your pains will disappear."

And the sick followed his words, for they knew that they would be healed.

And there were also other sick who suffered much from their pains, howbeit, they persisted in their fasting. And their force was spent, and great heat tormented them. And when they would have risen from their bed to go to Jesus, their heads began to turn, as if it were a gusty wind which shook them, and as oft as they tried to stand upon their feet, they fell back to the ground.

Then Jesus went to them and said: "You suffer, for Satan and his diseases torment your bodies. But fear not, for their power over you will quickly end. For Satan is like a choleric neighbor who entered his neighbor's house while he was absent, intending to take his goods away to his own house. But some told the other that his enemy was ravaging within his house, and he came back to his house, running. And when the wicked neighbor, having gathered together all that pleased him, saw from afar the master of the house returning in haste, then he was very wroth that he could not take all away, and set to breaking and spoiling all that was there, to destroy all. So that even if the things might not be his, the other might have nothing. But immediately the lord of the house came in, and before the wicked neighbor fulfilled his purpose, he took him and cast him out of the house. I tell you truly, even so did Satan enter your bodies which are the habitation of God. And he took in his power all that he wished to steal: your breath, your blood, your bone, your flesh, your bowels, your eyes, and your ears. But by your fasting and your prayer, you have called back the lord of your body and his angels. And now Satan sees that the true lord of your body returns, and that it is the end of his power. Wherefore, in his wrath he gathers his strength once again, that he may destroy your bodies before the coming of the lord. It is for this that Satan torments you so grievously, for he feels that the end is come. But let not your hearts tremble, for soon will the Angels of God appear, to occupy again their abodes and rededicate them as temples of God. And they will seize Satan and cast him from your bodies with all his diseases and all his uncleannesses. And happy will you be, for you will receive the reward of your steadfastness, and you will never see disease."

And there was among the sick, one that was more tormented by Satan than all the others. And his body was as parched as a skeleton, and his skin yellow as a falling leaf. He was so weak already that he could not, even upon his hands, crawl to Jesus, and cried only to him from afar: "Master, have pity on me, for never has man suffered, not from the beginning of the world, as I do suffer. I know that you are indeed sent by God, and I know that if you will, you can straightway cast out Satan from my body. Do not the Angels of God obey God's messenger? Come, Master, and cast out Satan from me now, for he rages angrily within me and grievous is his torment."

And Jesus answered him: "Satan torments you thus greatly because you have already fasted many days, and you do not pay to him his tribute. You do not feed him with all the abominations with which you hitherto defiled the temple of your spirit. You torment Satan with hunger, and so in his anger he torments you also. Fear not, for I tell you, Satan will be destroyed before your body is destroyed; for while you fast and pray, the Angels of God protect your body, that Satan's power may not destroy you. And the anger of Satan is impotent against the Angels of God."

Then they all came to Jesus and with loud cries besought him, saying: "Master, have compassion on him, for he suffers more than we all, and if you do not at once cast Satan out of him, we fear he will not live until tomorrow."

And Jesus answered them: "Great is your faith. Be it according to your faith, and you shall see soon, face to face, the frightful countenance of Satan, and the power of the Son of Man. For I will cast out from you the powerful Satan by the strength of the innocent lamb of God, the weakest creature of the Lord. For the holy spirit of God makes more powerful the weakest than the strongest."

And Jesus milked a ewe which was feeding among the grass. And he put the milk upon the sand made hot by the sun, saying: "Lo, the power of the Angel of Water has entered this milk. And now the power of the Angel of Sunshine will enter it also."

And the milk became hot by the strength of the sun.

"And now the Angels of Water and of Sun will join with the Angel of Air."

And lo, the vapor of the hot milk began to rise slowly into the air.

"Come and breathe in by your mouth the strength of the Angels of Water, of Sunshine, and of Air, that it may come into your body and cast out the Satan from you."

And the sick man whom Satan tormented did breathe within himself, deeply, the rising whitish vapor.

"Straightway will Satan leave your body, since for three days he starves and finds no food within you. He will come out of you to satisfy his hunger by the hot, steaming milk, for this food finds favor in his sight. He will smell its smell, and will not be able to resist the hunger which has tormented him three days already. But the Son of Man will destroy his body, that he may torment none else again."

Then the sick man's body was seized with an ague, and he retched as though he would vomit, but he could not. And he gasped for air, for his breath was spent. And he fainted on the lap of Jesus.

"Now does Satan leave his body. See him." And Jesus pointed to the sick man's opened mouth.

And then they all saw with astonishment and terror that Satan was coming out from his mouth in the shape of an abominable worm, straight towards the steaming milk. Then Jesus took two sharp stones in his hands and crushed the head of Satan, and drew out from the sick man all the body of the monster which was almost as long as the man. When the abominable worm came out of the sick man's throat, he recovered at once his breath, and then all his pains ceased. And the others looked with terror at the abominable body of Satan.

"See, what an abominable beast you carried and nourished in your body for long years. I have cast it out of you and killed it that it may never again torment you. Give thanks to God that his angels have made you free, and sin no more, lest Satan return to you again. Let your body be henceforth a temple dedicated to your God."

And they were all amazed at his words and at his power. And they said: "Master, you are indeed God's messenger, and do know all secrets."

"And you," answered Jesus, "be true Sons of God, that you also may partake in his power and in the knowledge of all secrets. For wisdom and power can come only from the love of God. Love, therefore, your Heavenly Father and your Earthly Mother with all your heart, and with all your spirit. And serve them, that their angels may serve you also. Let all your deeds be sacrificed to God. And feed not Satan, for the wages of sin is death. But with God lies the reward of the good, his love, which is knowledge and power of eternal life."

And they all knelt down to give thanks to God for his love.

And Jesus departed, saying: "I will come again to all who persist in prayer and fasting till the seventh day. Peace be with you."

And the sick man from whom Jesus had cast out the Satan, stood up, for the strength of life had come back to him. He breathed out deeply, and his eyes became clear, for every pain had left him. And he cast himself down upon the ground where Jesus had stood, and he kissed the print of his feet and he wept.

And it was by the bed of a stream, many sick fasted and prayed with God's angels for seven days and seven nights. And great was their reward, because they followed Jesus' words. And with the passing of the seventh day, all their pains left them. And when the sun rose over the earth's rim they saw Jesus coming towards them from the mountain, with the brightness of the rising sun about his head.

"Peace be with you."

And they said no word at all, but only cast themselves down before him, and touched the hem of his garment in token of their healing.

"Give thanks not to me, but to your Earthly Mother, who sent you her healing angels. Go, and sin no more, that you may never again see disease. And let the healing angels become your guardians."

But they answered him: "Whither should we go, Master, for with you are the words of eternal life? Tell us, what are the sins which we must shun, that we may nevermore see disease?"

Jesus answered: "Be it so according to your faith," and he sat down among them, saying:

"It was said to them of old time, 'Honor thy Heavenly Father and thy Earthly Mother, and do their commandments, that thy days may be long upon the earth.' And next afterward was given this commandment, 'Thou shalt not kill,' for life is given to all by God, and that which God has given, let not man take away. For I tell you truly, from one Mother proceeds all that lives upon the earth. Therefore, he who kills, kills his brother. And from him will the Earthly Mother turn away, and will pluck from him her quickening breasts. And he will be shunned by her angels, and Satan will have his dwelling in his body. And the flesh of slain beasts in his body will become his own tomb. For I tell you truly, he who kills, kills himself, and whoso eats the flesh of slain beasts, eats of the body of death. For in his blood every drop of their blood turns to poison; in his breath their breath to stink; in his flesh their flesh to boils; in his bones their bones to chalk; in his bowels their bowels to decay; in his eyes their eyes to scales; in his ears their ears to waxy issue. And their death will become his death. For only in the service of your Heavenly Father are your debts of seven years forgiven in seven clays. But Satan forgives you nothing and you must pay him for all. 'Eye for eye, tooth for tooth, hand for hand, foot for foot; burning for burning, wound for wound; life for life, death for death.' For the wages of sin is death. Kill not, neither eat the flesh of your innocent prey, lest you become the slaves of Satan. For that is the path of sufferings, and it leads unto death. But do the will of God, that his angels may serve you on the way of life. Obey, therefore, the words of God: 'Behold, I have given you every herb-bearing seed, which is upon the face of all the earth, and every tree, in which is the fruit of a tree yielding seed; to you it shall be for meat. And to every beast of the earth, and to every fowl of the air, and to everything that creepeth upon the earth, wherein there is breath of life, I give every green herb for meat. Also the milk of every thing that moveth and liveth upon earth shall be meat for you; even as the green herb have I given unto them, so I give their milk unto you. But flesh, and the blood which quickens it, shall ye not eat. And, surely, your spurting blood will I require, your blood wherein is your soul; I will require all slain beasts, and the souls of all slain men. For I the Lord thy God am a God strong and jealous, visiting the iniquity of the fathers upon the children unto the third and fourth generation of them that hate me; and showing mercy unto thousands of them that love me, and keep my commandments. Love the Lord thy God with all thy heart, and with all thy soul, and with all thy strength: this is the first and greatest commandment.' And the second is like unto it: 'Love thy neighbor as thyself.' There is none other commandment greater than these."

And after these words they all remained silent, save one, who called out: "What am I to do, Master, if I see a wild beast rend my brother in the forest? Shall I let my brother perish, or kill the wild beast? Shall not I thus transgress the Law?"

And Jesus answered: "It was said to them of old time: 'All beasts that move upon the earth, all the fish of the sea, and all the fowl of the air are given into thy power.' I tell you truly, of all creatures living upon the earth, God created only man after his image. Wherefore beasts are for man, and not man for beasts. You do not, therefore, transgress the Law if you kill the wild beast to save your brother's life. For I tell you truly, man is more than the beast. But he who kills the beast without a cause, though the beast attack him not, through lust for slaughter, or for its flesh, or for its hide, or yet for its tusks, evil is the deed which he does, for he is turned into a wild beast himself. Wherefore is his end also as the end of the wild beasts."

Then another said: "Moses, the greatest in Israel, suffered our forefathers to eat the flesh of clean beasts, and forbade only the flesh of unclean beasts. Why, therefore, do you forbid us the flesh of all beasts? Which law comes from God? That of Moses, or your law?"

And Jesus answered: "God gave, by Moses, ten commandments to your forefathers. 'These commandments are hard,' said your forefathers, and they could not keep them. When Moses saw this, he had compassion on his people, and would not that they perish. And then he gave them ten times ten commandments less hard, that they might follow them. For he whose feet are strong as the mountain of Zion, needs no crutches; but he whose limbs do shake, gets further having crutches, than without them. And Moses said to the Lord: 'My heart is filled with sorrow, for my people will be lost. For they are without knowledge, and are not able to understand thy commandments. They are as little children who cannot yet understand their father's words. Suffer, Lord, that I give them other laws, that they may not perish. If they may not be with thee, Lord, let them not be against thee; that they may sustain themselves, and when the time has come, and they are ripe for thy words, reveal to them thy laws.' For that did Moses break the two tablets of s tone whereon were written the ten commandments, and he gave them ten times ten in their stead. And of these ten times ten the Scribes and Pharisees have made a hundred times ten commandments. And they have laid unbearable burdens on your shoulders, that they themselves do not carry. For the more nigh are the commandments to God, the less do we need; and the farther they are from God, then the more do we need. Wherefore are the laws of the Pharisees and Scribes innumerable; the laws of the Son of Man seven; of the angels three; and of God one.

"Therefore, I teach you only those laws which you can understand, that you may become men, and follow the seven laws of the Son of Man. Then will the unknown Angels of the Heavenly Father also reveal their laws to you, that God's holy spirit may descend upon you, and lead you to his Law."

And all were astonished at his wisdom, and asked him: "Continue, Master, and teach us all the laws which we can receive."

And Jesus continued: "God commanded your forefathers: 'Thou shalt not kill.' But their heart was hardened and they killed. Then Moses desired that at least they should not kill men, and he suffered them to kill beasts. And then the heart of your forefathers was hardened yet more, and they killed men and beasts likewise. But I do say to you: Kill neither men, nor beasts, nor yet the food which goes into your mouth. For if you eat living food, the same will quicken you, but if you kill your food, the dead food will kill you also. For life comes only from life, and from death comes always death. For everything which kills your foods, kills your bodies also. And everything which kills your bodies, kills your souls also. And your bodies become what your foods are, even as your spirits, likewise, become what your thoughts are. Therefore, eat not anything which fire, or frost, or water has destroyed. For burned, frozen, and rotted foods will burn, freeze, and rot your body also. Be not like the foolish husbandman who sowed in his ground cooked, and frozen, and rotten seeds. And the autumn came, and his fields bore nothing. And great was his distress. But be like that husbandman who sowed in his field living seed, and whose field bore living ears of wheat, paying a hundredfold for the seeds which he planted. For I tell you truly, live only by the fire of life, and prepare not your foods with the fire of death, which kills your foods, your bodies, and your souls also."

"Master, where is the fire of life?" asked some of them.

"In you, in your blood, and in your bodies."

"And the fire of death?" asked others.

"It is the fire which blazes outside your body, which is hotter than your blood. With that fire of death, you cook your foods in your homes and in your fields. I tell you truly, it is the same fire which destroys your foods and your bodies, even as the fire of malice, which ravages your thoughts, ravages your spirits. For your body is that which you eat, and your spirit is that which you think. Eat nothing, therefore, which a stronger fire than the fire of life has killed. Wherefore, prepare and eat all fruits of trees, and all grasses of the fields, and all milk of beasts good for eating. For all these are fed and ripened by the fire of life; all are the gift of the Angels of our Earthly Mother. But eat nothing to which only the fire of death gives savor, for such is of Satan."

"How should we cook our daily bread without fire, Master?" asked some with great astonishment.

"Let the Angels of God prepare your bread. Moisten your wheat, that the Angel of Water may enter it. Then set it in the air, that the Angel of Air also may embrace it. And leave it from morning to evening beneath the sun, that the Angel of Sunshine may descend upon it. And the blessing of the three angels will soon make the germ of life to sprout in your wheat. Then crush your grain, and make thin wafers, as did your forefathers when they departed out of Egypt, the house of bondage. Put them back again beneath the sun from its appearing, and when it is risen to its highest in the heavens, turn them over on the other side that they be embraced there also by the Angel of Sunshine, and leave them there until the sun be set. For the Angels of Water, of Air, and of Sunshine fed and ripened the wheat in the field, and they, likewise, must prepare also your bread. And the same sun which, with the fire of life, made the wheat to grow and ripen, must cook your bread with the same fire. For the fire of the sun gives life to the wheat, to the bread, and to the body. But the fire of death kills the wheat, the bread, and the body. And the living Angels of the living God serve only living men. For God is the God of the living, and not the God of the dead.

"So eat always from the table of God: the fruits of the trees, the grain and grasses of the field, the milk of beasts, and the honey of bees. For everything beyond these is of Satan, and leads by the way of sins and of diseases unto death. But the foods which you eat from the abundant table of God give strength and youth to your body, and you will never see diseases For the table of God fed Methuselah of old, and I tell you truly, if you live even as he lived, then will the God of the living give you also long life upon the earth as was his.

"For I tell you truly, the God of the living is richer than all the rich of the earth, and his abundant table is richer than the richest table of feasting of all the rich upon the earth. Eat, therefore, all your life at the table of our Earthly Mother, and you will never see want. And when you eat at her table, eat all things even as they are found on the table of the Earthly Mother. Cook not, neither mix all things one with another, lest your bowels become as steaming bogs. For I tell you truly, this is abominable in the eyes of the Lord.

"And be not like the greedy servant, who always ate up, at the table of his lord, the portions of others. And he devoured everything himself, and mixed all together in his gluttony. And seeing that, his lord was wroth with him, and drove him from the table. And when all had ended their meal, he mixed together all that remained upon the table, and called the greedy servant to him, and said: 'Take and eat all this with the swine, for your place is with them, and not at my table.'

"Take heed, therefore, and defile not with all kinds of abominations the temple of your bodies. Be content with two or three sorts of food, which you will find always upon the table of our Earthly Mother. And desire not to devour all things which you see around you. For I tell you truly, if you mix together all sorts of food in your body, then the peace of your body will cease, and endless war will rage in you. And it will be blotted out even as homes and kingdoms divided against themselves work their own destruction. For your God is the God of peace, and does never help division. Arouse not, therefore, against you the wrath of God, lest he drive you from his table, and lest you be compelled to go to the table of Satan, where the fire of sins, diseases, and death will corrupt your body.

"And when you eat, never eat unto fullness. Flee the temptations of Satan, and listen to the voice of God's angels. For Satan and his power tempt you always to eat more and more. But live by the spirit, and resist the desires of the body. And your fasting is always pleasing in the eyes of the Angels of God. So give heed to how much you have eaten when your body is sated, and always eat less by a third.

"Let the weight of your daily food be not less than a mina, but mark that it go not beyond two. Then will the Angels of God serve you always, and you will never fall into the bondage of Satan and of his diseases. Trouble not the work of the angels in your body by eating often. For I tell you truly, he who eats more than twice in the day does in him the work of Satan. And the Angels of God leave his body, and soon Satan will take possession of it. Eat only when the sun is highest in the heavens, and again when it is set. And you will never see disease, for such finds favor in the eyes of the Lord. And if you will that the Angels of God rejoice in your body, and that Satan shun you afar, then sit but once in the day at the table of God. And then your days will be long upon the earth, for this is pleasing in the eyes of the Lord. Eat always when the table of God is served before you, and eat always of that which you find upon the table of God. For I tell you truly, God knows well what your body needs, and when it needs.

"From the coming of the month of Ijar, eat barley; from the month of Sivan, eat wheat, the most perfect among all seed-bearing herbs. And let your daily bread be made of wheat, that the Lord may take care of your bodies. From Tammuz, eat the sour grape, that your body may diminish, and Satan may depart from it. In the month of Elul, gather the grape that the juice may serve you as drink. In the month of Marchesvan, gather the sweet grape, dried and sweetened by the Angel of Sun, that your bodies may increase, for the Angels of the Lord dwell in them. You should eat figs rich in juice in the months of Ab and Shebat, and what remain, let the Angel of Sun keep them for you; eat them with the meat of almonds in all the months when the trees bear no fruits. And the herbs which come after rain, these eat in the month of Thebet, that your blood may be cleansed of all your sins. And in the same month begin to eat also the milk of your beasts, because for this did the Lord give the herbs of the fields to all the beasts which render milk, that they might with their milk feed man. For I tell you truly, happy are they that eat only at the table of God, and eschew all the abominations of Satan. Eat not unclean foods brought from far countries, but eat always that which your trees bear. For your God knows well what is needful for you, and where and when. And he gives to all peoples of all kingdoms for food that which is best for each. Eat not as the heathen do, who stuff themselves in haste, defiling their bodies with all manner of abominations.

"For the power of God's angels enters into you with the living food which the Lord gives you from his royal table. And when you eat, have above you the Angel of Air, and below you the Angel of Water. Breathe long and deeply at all your meals, that the Angel of Air may bless your repasts. And chew well your food with your teeth, that it become water, and that the Angel of Water turn it into blood in your body. And eat slowly, as it were a prayer you make to the Lord. For I tell you truly, the power of God enters into you, if you eat after this manner at his table. But Satan turns into a steaming bog the body of him upon whom the Angels of Air and Water do not descend at his repasts. And the Lord suffers him no longer at his table. For the table of the Lord is an altar, and he who eats at the table of God is in a temple. For I tell you truly, the body of the Son of Man is turned into a temple, and his inwards into an altar, if he does the commandments of God. Wherefore, put naught upon the altar of the Lord when your spirit is vexed, neither think upon any one with anger in the temple of God. And enter only into the Lord's sanctuary when you feel in yourselves the call of his angels, for all that you eat in sorrow, or in anger, or without desire, becomes a poison in your body. For the breath of Satan defiles all these. Place with joy your offerings upon the altar of your body, and let all evil thoughts depart from you when you receive into your body the power of God from his table. And never sit at the table of God before he call you by the Angel of Appetite.

"Rejoice, therefore, always with God's angels at their royal table, for this is pleasing to the heart of the Lord. And your life will be long upon the earth, for the most precious of God's servants will serve you all your days: the Angel of Joy.

"And forget not that every seventh day is holy and consecrated to God. On six days feed your body with the gifts of the Earthly Mother, but on the seventh day sanctify your body for your Heavenly Father. On the seventh day eat not any earthly food, but live only on the words of God, and be all the day with the Angels of the Lord in the kingdom of the Heavenly Father. And on the seventh day let the Angels of God build the kingdom of the heavens in your body, as you labor for six days in the kingdom of the Earthly Mother. And let not food trouble the work of the Angels in your body throughout the seventh day. And God will give you long life upon earth, that you may have life everlasting in the kingdom of the heavens. For I tell you truly, if you see not diseases any more upon earth, you will live forever in the kingdom of the heavens.

"And God will send you each morning the Angel of Sunshine to wake you from your sleep. Therefore, obey your Heavenly Father's summons, and lie not idle in your beds, for the Angels of Air and Water await you already without. And labor all day long with the Angels of the Earthly Mother that you may come to know them and their works ever more and more well. But when the sun is set, and your Heavenly Father sends you his most precious angel, sleep, then take your rest, and be all the night with the Angel of Sleep. And then will your Heavenly Father send you his unknown angels, that they may be with you the livelong night. And the Heavenly Father's unknown angels will teach you many things concerning the kingdom of God, even as the angels that you know of the Earthly Mother, instruct you in the things of her kingdom. For I tell you truly, you will be every night the guests of the kingdom of your Heavenly Father, if you do his commandments. And when you wake up upon the morrow, you will feel in you the power of the unknown angels. And your Heavenly Father will send them to you every night, that they may build your spirit, even as every day the Earthly Mother sends you her angels, that they may build your body. For I tell you truly, if in the daytime your Earthly Mother folds you in her arms, and in the night the Heavenly Father breathes his kiss upon you, then will the Sons of Men become the Sons of God.

"Resist day and night the temptations of Satan. Wake not by night, neither sleep by day, lest the Angels of God depart from you.

"And take no delight in any drink, nor in any smoke from Satan, waking you by night and making you to sleep by day. For I tell you truly, all the drinks and smokes of Satan are abominations in the eyes of your God.

"Commit not whoredom, by night or by day, for the whoremonger is like a tree whose sap runs out from its trunk. And that tree will be dried up before its time, nor will it ever bear fruit. Therefore, go not a-whoring, lest Satan dry up your body, and the Lord make your seed unfruitful.

"Shun all that is too hot and too cold. For it is the will of your Earthly Mother that neither heat nor cold should harm your body. And let not your bodies become either hotter or colder than as God's angels warm or cool them. And if you do the commandments of the Earthly

Mother, then as oft as your body becomes too hot, will she send the Angel of Coolness to cool you, and as oft as your body becomes too cold, will she send you the Angel of Heat to warm you again.

"Follow the example of all the Angels of the Heavenly Father and of the Earthly Mother, who work day and night, without ceasing, upon the kingdoms of the heavens and of the earth. Therefore, receive also into yourselves the strongest of God's Angels, the Angel of Deeds, and work all together upon the kingdom of God. Follow the example of the running water, the wind as it blows, the rising and setting of the sun, the growing plants and trees, the beasts as they run and gambol, the wane and waxing of the moon, the stars as they come and go again; all these do move, and do perform their labors. For all which has life does move, and only that which is dead is still. And God is the God of the living, and Satan that of the dead. Serve, therefore, the living God, that the eternal movement of life may sustain you, and that you may escape the eternal stillness of death. Work, therefore, without ceasing, to build the kingdom of God, lest you be cast into the kingdom of Satan. For eternal joy abounds in the living kingdom of God, but still sorrow darkens the kingdom of death of Satan. Be, therefore, true Sons of your Earthly Mother and of your Heavenly Father, that you fall not as slaves of Satan. And your Earthly Mother and Heavenly Father will send you their angels to teach, to love, and to serve you. And their angels will write the commandments of God in your head, in your heart, and in your hands, that you may know, feel, and do God's commandments.

"And pray every day to your Heavenly Father and Earthly mother, that your soul become as perfect as your Heavenly Father's holy spirit is perfect, and that your body become as perfect as the body of your Earthly Mother is perfect. For if you understand, feel, and do the commandments, then all for which you pray to your Heavenly Father and your Earthly Mother will be given you. For the wisdom, the love, and the power of God are above all.

"After this manner, therefore, pray to your Heavenly Father: Our Father which art in heaven, hallowed be thy name. Thy kingdom come. Thy will be done on earth as it is in heaven. Give us this day our daily bread. And forgive us our debts, as we forgive our debtors. And lead us not into temptation, but deliver us from evil. For thine is the kingdom, the power, and the glory, forever. Amen.

"And after this manner pray to your Earthly Mother: Our Mother which art upon earth, hallowed be thy name. Thy kingdom come, and thy will be done in us, as it is in thee. As thou sendest every day thy angels, send them to us also. Forgive us our sins, as we atone all our sins against thee. And lead us not into sickness, but deliver us from all evil, for thine is the earth, the body, and the health. Amen."

And they all prayed together with Jesus to the Heavenly Father and to the Earthly Mother.

And afterwards Jesus spoke thus to them: "Even as your bodies have been reborn through the Earthly Mother's angels, may your spirit, likewise, be reborn through the Angels of the Heavenly Father. Become, therefore, true Sons of your Father and of your Mother, and true Brothers of the Sons of Men. Till now you were at war with your Father, with your Mother, and with your Brothers. And you have served Satan. From today live at peace with your Heavenly Father, and with your Earthly Mother, and with your Brothers, the Sons of Men. And fight only against Satan, lest he rob you of your peace. I give the peace of your Earthly Mother to your body, and the peace of your Heavenly Father to your spirit. And let the peace of both reign among the Sons of Men.

"Come to me, all that are weary and that suffer in strife and affliction! For my peace will strengthen you and comfort you. For my peace is exceeding full of joy. Wherefore do I always greet you after this manner: 'Peace be with you!' Do you always, therefore, so greet one another, that upon your body may descend the peace of your Earthly Mother, and upon your spirit the peace of your Heavenly Father. And then you will find peace also among yourselves, for the kingdom of God is within you. And now return to your Brothers with whom hitherto you were at war, and give your peace to them also. For happy are they that strive for peace, for they will find the peace of God. Go, and sin no more. And give to everyone your peace, even as I have given my peace unto you. For my peace is of God. Peace be with you."

And he left them.

And his peace descended upon them; and in their heart the Angel of Love, in their head the wisdom of Law, and in their hands the power of rebirth, they went forth among the Sons of Men, to bring the light of peace to those that warred in darkness.

And they parted, wishing one to another:

"PEACE BE WITH YOU."

THE ESSENE GOSPEL OF PEACE
Book Two
The Unknown Books of The Essenes

CONTENTS

Preface 47

Introduction 49

THE VISION OF ENOCH, the most ancient revelation

God Speaks to Man 55

FROM THE ESSENE BOOK OF MOSES

The Ten Commandments 61

THE COMMUNIONS 67

Communions with the Angels of the Earthly Mother

The Angel of Sun 70
The Angel of Water 70
The Angel of Air 71
The Angel of Earth 72
The Angel of Life 73
The Angel of Joy 74
The Earthly Mother 74

Communions with the Angels of the Heavenly Father

The Angel of Power 77
The Angel of Love 78
The Angel of Wisdom 79
The Angel of Eternal Life 81

The Angel of Work..82

The Angel of Peace.. 83

The Heavenly Father.. 84

FROM THE ESSENE BOOK OF JESUS

The Sevenfold Peace.. 87

Peace with the Body.. 90

Peace with the Mind.. 92

Peace with the Brotherhood.. 93

Peace with Mankind.. 94

Peace with the Wisdom of the Ages............................. 96

Peace with the Kingdom of the Earthly Mother.................98

Peace with the Kingdom of the Heavenly Father............... 100

Fragments Identical with the Dead Sea Scrolls.................. 105

From The Essene Book of the Teacher of Righteousness...... 111

From The Essene Gospel of John................................. 117

From The Essene Book of Revelations........................... 121

PREFACE

Book Two of the Essene Gospel of Peace

I have to begin this preface with a great confession: this is not my first translation of Book Two of the Essene Gospel of Peace; it is my second. The first effort took many years to complete, and it was composed painstakingly and literally, with hundreds of cross references and abundant philological and exegetical footnotes. When it was finished, I was very proud of it, and in a glow of self-satisfied accomplishment, I gave it to my friend, Aldous Huxley, to read. Two weeks later, I asked him what he thought of my monumental translation. "It is very, very bad, he answered. "It is even worse than the most boring treatises of the patristics and scholastics, which nobody reads today. It is so dry and uninteresting, in fact, that I have no desire to read Book Three." I was speechless, so he continued. "You should rewrite it, and give it some of the vitality of your other books—make it literary, readable, and attractive for twentieth century readers. I'm sure the Essenes did not speak to each other in footnotes! In the form it is in now, the only readers you will have for it may be a few dogmatists in theological seminaries, who seem to take masochistic pleasure in reading this sort of thing. However," he added with a smile, "you might find some value in it as a cure for insomnia; each time I tried to read it I fell asleep in a few minutes. You might try to sell a few copies that way by advertising a new sleep remedy in the health magazines—no harmful chemicals, and all that."

It took me a long time to recuperate from his criticism. I put aside the manuscript for years. Meanwhile, I continued to receive thousands of letters from many readers from all parts of the world of my translation of Book One of the Essene Gospel of Peace, asking for the second and third books promised in the preface. Finally, I got the courage to start again. The passing of the years had mellowed my attitude and I saw my friend's criticism in a new light. I rewrote the entire manuscript, treating it as literature and poetry, coming to grips with the great problems of life, both ancient and contemporary. It was not easy to be faithful to the original, and at the same time to present the eternal truths in a way that would appeal to twentieth century man. And yet, it was vitally important that I try; for the Essenes, above all others, strove to win the hearts of men through reason, and the powerful and vivid example of their lives.

Sadly, Aldous is no longer here to read my second translation. I have a feeling he would have liked it (not a single footnote!), but I will have to leave the final judgment to my readers. If Books Two and Three will become as popular as Book One, my efforts of many, many years will be amply rewarded.

San Diego, California
the first of November, 1974.

EDMOND BORDEAUX SZEKELY

INTRODUCTION

There are three paths leading to Truth. The first is the path of the consciousness, the second that of nature, and the third is the accumulated experience of past generations, which we receive in the shape of the great masterpieces of all ages. From time immemorial, man and humanity have followed all three paths.

The first path to Truth, the path of the consciousness, is that followed by the great mystics. They consider that the consciousness is the most immediate reality for us and is the key to the universe. It is something which is in us, which *is* us. And throughout the ages the mystics have made the discovery that the laws of human consciousness contain an aspect not found in the laws governing the material universe.

A certain dynamic unity exists in our consciousness, where one is at the same time many. It is possible for us to have simultaneously different thoughts, ideas, associations, images, memories and intuitions occupying our consciousness within fragments of a minute or a second, yet all this multiplicity will still constitute only a single dynamic unity. Therefore, the laws of mathematics, which are valid for the material universe and are a key to its understanding, will not be valid in the field of consciousness, a realm where two and two do not necessarily make four. The mystics also found that measurements of space, time, and weight, universally valid in nature and throughout the material universe, are not applicable to the consciousness, where sometimes a few seconds seem like hours, or hours like a minute.

Our consciousness does not exist in space and therefore cannot be measured in spatial terms. It has its own time, which is very often timelessness, so temporal measurements cannot be applied to Truth reached by this path. The great mystics discovered that the human consciousness, besides being the most immediate and the inmost reality for us, is at the same time our closest source of energy, harmony, and knowledge. The path to Truth leading to and through the consciousness produced the great teachings of humanity, the great intuitions and the great masterpieces throughout the ages. Such then is the first path to or source of Truth, as the Essene traditions understand and interpret it.

Unfortunately, the magnificent original intuitions of the great masters often lose their vitality as they pass down the generations. They are very often modified, distorted, and turned into dogmas, and all too frequently their values become petrified in institutions and organized hierarchies. The pure intuitions are choked by the sands of time, and eventually have to be dug out by seekers of Truth able to penetrate into their essence.

Another danger is that persons following this path to Truth, the path of the consciousness—may fall into exaggerations. They come to think that this is the only path to Truth and disregard all others. Very often, too, they apply the specific laws of the human consciousness to the material universe where they lack validity and ignore the laws proper to the latter sphere. The mystic often creates for himself an artificial universe, farther and farther removed from reality, till he ends by living in an ivory tower, having lost all contact with reality and life.

The second of the three paths is the path of nature. While the first path of the consciousness starts from within and penetrates thence into the totality of things, the second path takes the opposite way. Its starting point is the external world. It is the path of the scientist and has been followed in all ages through experience and through experiment, through the use of inductive and deductive methods. The scientist, working with exact quantitative measurements, measures everything in space and time, and makes all possible correlations.

With his telescope he penetrates into far-distant cosmic space, into the various solar and galactic systems; through spectrum analysis he measures the constituents of the different planets in cosmic space; and by mathematical calculation he establishes in advance the movements of celestial bodies. Applying the law of cause and effect, the scientist establishes a long chain of causes and effects which help him to explain and measure the universe, as well as life.

But the scientist, like the mystic, sometimes falls into exaggerations. While science has transformed the life of mankind and has created great values, for man in all ages, it has failed to give entire satisfaction in the solution of the final problems of existence, life, and the universe. The scientist has the long chain of causes and effects secure in all its particles, but he has no idea what to do with the end of the chain. He has no solid point to which he may attach the end of the chain, and so, by the path to Truth through nature and the material universe, he is unable to answer the great and eternal questions concerning the beginning and end of all things.

The greatest scientists recognize that in the metaphysical field beyond the scientific chain there is something else—continuing from the end of that chain. However, there are also the dogmatic scientists who deny any other approach to Truth than their own, who refuse to attribute reality to the facts and phenomena which they cannot fit neatly into their own categories and classifications.

The path to Truth through nature is not that of the dogmatic scientist, just as the first path is not that of the one-sided mystic. Nature is a great open book in which everything can be found, if we learn to draw from it the inspiration which it has given to the great thinkers of all ages. If we learn her language, nature will reveal to us all the laws of life and the universe.

It is for this reason that all the great masters of humanity from time to time withdrew into nature: Zarathustra and Moses into the mountains, Buddha to the forest, Jesus and the Essenes to the desert—and thus followed this second path as well as that of the consciousness. The two paths do not contradict one another, but harmoniously complete one another in full knowledge of the laws of both. It was thus that the great teachers reached wonderful and deeply profound truths which have given inspiration to millions through thousands of years.

The third path to Truth, is the wisdom, knowledge, and experience acquired by the great thinkers of all ages and transmitted to us in the form of great teachings, the great sacred books or scriptures, and the great masterpieces of universal literature which together form what today we would call universal culture. In brief, therefore, our approach to Truth is a threefold one: through consciousness, nature, and culture.

In the following chapters we shall follow this threefold path leading to Truth and shall examine and translate some of the great sacred writings of the Essenes.

There are different ways of studying these great writings. One way—the way of all theologians and of the organized Churches—is to consider each text literally. This is the dogmatic way resulting from a long process of petrification, by which truths are inevitably transformed into dogmas.

When the theologian follows this most easy but one-sided path, he runs into endless contradictions and complications, and he reaches a conclusion as far removed from the truth as that of the scientific interpreter of these texts who rejects them as entirely valueless and without validity. The approaches of the dogmatic theologian and the exclusivist scientist represent two extremes.

A third error is to believe, as do certain symbolists, that these books have no more than a symbolic content and are nothing more than parables. With their own particular way of exaggeration these symbolists make thousands of different and quite contradictory interpretations of these great texts. The spirit of the Essene traditions is opposed to all three of these ways of interpreting these ageless writings and follows an entirely different approach.

The Essene method of interpretation of these books is, on the one hand, to place them in harmonious correlation with the laws of the human consciousness and of nature, and, on the other, to consider the facts and circumstances of the age and environment in which they were written. This approach also takes into account the degree of evolution and understanding of the people to whom the particular master was addressing his message.

Since all the great masters had to adapt their teaching to the level of their audience, they found it necessary to formulate both an exoteric and esoteric teaching. The exoteric message was one comprehensible to the people at large and was expressed in terms of various rules, forms, and rituals corresponding to the basic needs of the people and the age concerned. Parallel with this, the esoteric teachings have survived through the ages partly as written and partly as unwritten living traditions, free from forms, rituals, rules and dogmas, and in all periods have been kept alive and practiced by a small minority.

It is in this spirit of the interpretation of the Truth that the Essene Gospel of Peace will be translated in the following pages. Rejecting the dogmatic methods of literal and purely scientific interpretation.

as well as the exaggeration of the symbolists, we shall try to translate the Essene Gospel of Peace in the light of our consciousness and of nature, and in harmony with the great traditions of the Essenes, to whose brotherhood the authors of the Dead Sea Scrolls themselves belonged.

THE VISION OF ENOCH

THE MOST ANCIENT REVELATION

God Speaks to Man

I speak to you.
Be still
Know
I am
God.

I spoke to you
When you were born.
Be still
Know
I am
God.

I spoke to you
At your first sight.
Be still
Know
I am
God.

I spoke to you
At your first word.
Be still
Know
I am
God.

I spoke to you
At your first thought.
Be still
Know
I am
God.

I spoke to you
At your first love.
Be still
Know
I am
God.

I spoke to you
At your first song.
Be still
Know I am
God.

I speak to you
Through the grass of the meadows.
Be still
Know
I am
God.

I speak to you
Through the trees of the forests.
Be still
Know
I am
God.

I speak to you
Through the valleys
and the hills.
Be still
Know
I am
God.

I speak to you
Through the Holy Mountains.
Be still
Know
I am
God.

I speak to you
Through the rain and the snow.
Be still
Know
I am
God.

I speak to you
Through the waves of the sea.
Be still
Know
I am
God.

I speak to you
Through the dew of the morning.
Be still
Know

I am
God.

I speak to you
Through the peace of the evening.
Be still
Know
I am
God.

I speak to you
Through the splendor of the sun.
Be still
Know
I am
God

I speak to you
Through the brilliant stars.
Be still
Know
I am
God.

I speak to you
Through the storm and the clouds.
Be still
Know
I am
God.

I speak to you
Through the thunder and lightning.
Be still

*Know
I am
God*

*I speak to you
Through the mysterious rainbow.
Be still
Know
I am
God.*

*I will speak to you
When you are alone.
Be still
Know
I am
God*

*I will speak to you
Through the Wisdom of the Ancients.
Be still
Know
I am
God*

*I will speak to you
At the end of time.
Be still
Know
I am
God.*

*I will speak to you
When you have seen my Angels.*

*Be still
Know
I am
God.*

*I will speak to you
Throughout Eternity.
Be still
Know
I am
God*

*I speak to you.
Be still
Know
I am
God.*

FROM THE ESSENE BOOK OF MOSES

THE TEN COMMANDMENTS

And Mount Sinai was altogether in smoke because the Lord descended upon it in fire. And the smoke thereof ascended as the smoke of a furnace, and the whole mount quaked greatly.

And the Lord came down upon Mount Sinai, on the top of the mount. And the Lord called Moses up to the top of the mount. And Moses went up.

And the Lord called unto Moses out of the mountain, saying, "Come unto me, for I would give thee the Law for thy people, which shall be a covenant for the Children of Light."

And Moses went up unto God. And God spake all these words, saying,

I am the Law, thy God, which hath brought thee out from the depths of the bondage of darkness.

Thou shalt have no other Laws before me.

Thou shalt not make unto thee any image of the Law in heaven above or in the earth beneath. I am the invisible Law, without beginning and without end.

Thou shalt not make unto thee false laws, for I am the Law, and the whole Law of all laws. If thou forsake me, thou shalt be visited by disasters for generation upon generation.

If thou keepest my commandments, thou shalt enter the Infinite

Garden where stands the Tree of Life in the midst of the Eternal Sea.

Thou shalt not violate the Law. The Law is thy God, who shall not hold thee guiltless.

Honor thy Earthly Mother, that thy days may be long upon the land, and honor thy Heavenly Father, that eternal life be thine in the heavens, for the earth and the heavens are given unto thee by the Law, which is thy God.

Thou shalt greet thy Earthly Mother on the morning of the Sabbath.

Thou shalt greet the Angel of Earth on the second morning.

Thou shalt greet the Angel of Life on the third morning.

Thou shalt greet the Angel of Joy on the fourth morning.

Thou shalt greet the Angel of Sun on the fifth morning.

Thou shalt greet the Angel of Water on the sixth morning,

Thou shalt greet the Angel of Air on the seventh morning

All these Angels of the Earthly Mother shalt thou greet, and consecrate thyself to them, that thou mayest enter the Infinite Garden where stands the Tree of Life.

Thou shalt worship thy Heavenly Father on the evening of the Sabbath.

Thou shalt commune with the Angel of Eternal Life on the second evening.

Thou shalt commune with the Angel of Work on the third evening.

Thou shalt commune with the Angel of Peace on the fourth evening.

Thou shalt commune with the Angel of Power on the fifth evening,

Thou shalt commune with the Angel of Love on the sixth evening.

Thou shalt commune with the Angel of Wisdom on the seventh evening.

All these Angels of the Heavenly Father shalt thou commune with, that thy soul may bathe in the Fountain of Light and enter into the Sea of Eternity.

The seventh day is the Sabbath: thou shalt remember it, keep it holy. The Sabbath is the day of the Light of the Law, thy God. In it thou shalt not do any work, but search the Light, the Kingdom of thy God, and all things shall be given unto thee.

For know ye that during six days thou shalt work with the angels, but the seventh day shalt thou dwell in the Light of thy Lord, who is the holy Law.

Thou shalt not take the life from any living thing. Life comes only from God, who giveth it and taketh it away.

Thou shalt not debase Love. It is the sacred gift of thy Heavenly Father.

Thou shalt not trade thy Soul, the priceless gift of the loving God, for the riches of the world, which are as seeds sown on stony ground, having no root in themselves, and so endure but for a little while.

Thou shalt not be a false witness of the Law, to use it against thy brother: Only God knoweth the beginning and the ending of all things, for his eye is single, and he is the holy Law.

Thou shalt not covet thy neighbor's possessions. The Law giveth unto thee much greater gifts, even the earth and the heavens, if thou keep the Commandments of the Lord thy God.

And Moses heard the voice of the Lord and sealed within him the covenant that was between the Lord and the Children of Light.

And Moses turned, and went down from the mount, and the two tablets of the Law were in his hand.

And the tablets were the work of God, and the writing was the writing of God, graven upon the tablets.

And the people knew not what became of Moses, and they gathered themselves together and brake off their golden earrings and made a molten calf. And they worshipped unto the idol, and offered to it burnt offerings.

And they ate and drank and danced before the golden calf, which they had made, and they abandoned themselves to corruption and evil before the Lord.

And it came to pass, as soon as he came nigh unto the camp, that he saw the calf, and the dancing, and the wickedness of the people: and Moses' anger waxed hot, and he cast the tablets out of his hands, and brake them beneath the mount.

And it came to pass on the morrow, that Moses said unto the people, "Ye have sinned a great sin, ye have denied thy Creator. I will go up unto the Lord and plead atonement for thy sin.

And Moses returned unto the Lord, and said, "Lord, thou hast seen the desecration of thy Holy Law. For thy children lost faith, and worshipped the darkness, and made for themselves a golden calf. Lord, forgive them, for they are blind to the light."

And the Lord said unto Moses, *"Behold, at the beginning of time was a covenant made between God and man, and the holy flame of the Creator did enter unto him. And he was made the son of God, and it was given him to guard his inheritance of the firstborn, and to make fruitful the land of his Father and keep it holy. And he who casteth out the Creator from him doth spit upon his birthright, and no more grievous sin doth exist in the eyes of God."*

And the Lord spoke, saying, *"Only the Children of Light can keep the Commandments of the Law. Hear me, for I say thus: the tablets which thou didst break, these shall nevermore be written in the words of men. As thou didst return them to the earth and fire, so shall they live, invisible, in the hearts of those who are able to follow their Law. To thy people of little faith, who did sin against the Creator, even whilst thou stood on holy ground before thy God, -I will give another Law. It shall be a stem law, yea, it shall bind them, for they know not yet the Kingdom of Light."*

And Moses hid the invisible Law within his breast, and kept it for a sign to the Children of Light. And God gave unto Moses the written Law for the people, and he went down unto them, and spake unto them with a heavy heart.

And Moses said unto the people, "These are the laws which thy God hath given thee."

Thou shalt have no other gods before me.
Thou shalt not make unto thee any graven image.
Thou shalt not take the name of the Lord thy God in vain.
Remember the Sabbath day, to keep it holy.
Honor thy father and thy mother.
Thou shalt not kill.
Thou shalt not commit adultery.
Thou shalt not steal.
Thou shalt not bear false witness against thy neighbor.
Thou shalt not covet thy neighbor's house,
nor thy neighbor's wife, nor anything that is thy neighbor's.

And there was a day of mourning and atonement for the great sin against the Creator, which did not end. And the broken tablets of the Invisible Law lived hidden in the breast of Moses, until it came to pass that the Children of Light appeared in the desert, and the angels walked the earth.

THE COMMUNIONS

And it was by the bed of a stream, that the weary and afflicted came again to seek out Jesus. And like children, they had forgotten the Law; and like children, they sought out their father to show them where they had erred, and to set their feet again upon the path. And when the sun rose over the earth's rim they saw Jesus coming toward them from the mountain, with the brightness of the rising sun about his head.

And he raised his hand and smiled upon them, saying, "Peace be with you."

But they were ashamed to return his greeting, for each in his own way had turned his back on the holy teachings, and the Angels of the Earthly Mother and the Heavenly Father were not with them. And one man looked up in anguish and spoke: "Master, we are in sore need of your wisdom. For we know that which is good, and yet we follow evil. We know that to enter the Kingdom of Heaven we must walk with the Angels of the Day and of the Night, yet our feet walk in the ways of the wicked. The light of day shines only on our pursuit of pleasure, and the night falls on our heedless stupor. Tell us, Master, how may we talk with the angels, and stay within their holy circle, that the Law may burn in our hearts with a constant flame?"

And Jesus spoke to them:

"To lift your eyes to heaven
When all men's eyes are on the ground,
Is not easy.
To worship at the feet of the angels,
When all men worship only fame and riches,
Is not easy.

But the most difficult of all
Is to think the thoughts of the angels,
To speak the words of the angels,
And to do as angels do."

And one man spoke: "But, Master, we are but men, we are not angels. How then can we hope to walk in their ways? Tell us what we must do."

And Jesus spoke:

"As the son inherits the land of his father,
So have we inherited a Holy Land
From our Fathers.
This land is not a field to be ploughed,
But a place within us
Where we may build our Holy Temple.
And even as a temple must be raised,
Stone by stone,
So will I give to you those stones
For the building of the Holy Temple;
That which we have inherited
From our Fathers,
And their Fathers' Fathers."

And all the men gathered around Jesus, and their faces shone with desire to hear the words which would come from his lips. And he lifted his face to the rising sun, and the radiance of its rays filled his eyes as he spoke:

"The Holy Temple can be built
Only with the ancient Communions,
Those which are spoken,
Those which are thought,

And those which are lived.
For if they are spoken only with the mouth,
They are as a dead hive
Which the bees have forsaken,
That gives no more honey.
The Communions are a bridge
Between man and the angels,
And like a bridge,
Can be built only with patience,
Yea, even as the bridge over the river
Is fashioned stone by stone,
As they are found by the water's edge.

And the Communions are fourteen in number
As the Angels of the Heavenly Father
Number seven,
And the Angels of the Earthly Mother
Number seven.
And just as the roots of the tree
Sink into the earth and are nourished,
And the branches of the tree
Raise their arms to heaven,
So is man like the trunk of the tree,
With his roots deep
In the breast of his Earthly Mother,
And his soul ascending
To the bright stars of his Heavenly Father.
And the roots of the tree
Are the Angels of the Earthly Mother,
And the branches of the tree
Are the Angels of the Heavenly Father.
And this is the sacred Tree of Life
Which stands in the Sea of Eternity.

*The first Communion is with the Angel of Sun,
She who cometh each morning
As a bride from her chamber,
To shed her golden light on the world.
O thou immortal, shining, swift-steeded
Angel of the Sun!
There is no warmth without thee,
No fire without thee,
No life without thee.
As green leaves of the trees
Do worship thee,
And through thee is the tiny wheat kernel
Become a river of golden grass,
Moving with the wind.
Through thee is opened the flower
In the center of my body.
Therefore will I never hide myself
From thee.
Angel of Sun,
Holy messenger of the Earthly Mother,
Enter the holy temple within me
And give me the Fire of Life!
The second Communion is with The Angel of Water,
She who makes the rain
To fall on the arid plain,
Who fills the dry well to overflowing.
Yea, we do worship thee,
Water of Life.
From the heavenly sea
The waters run and flow forward
From the never-failing springs.
In my blood flow
A thousand pure springs,*

*And vapors, and clouds,
And all the waters
That spread over all the seven Kingdoms.*

*All the waters
The Creator hath made Are holy.
The voice of the Lord
Is upon the waters:
The God of Glory thundereth;
The Lord is upon many waters.
Angel of Water,
Holy messenger of the Earthly Mother,
Enter the blood that flows through me,
Wash my body in the rain
That falls from heaven,
And give me the Water of Life!*

*The third Communion is with
The Angel of Air,
Who spreads the perfume
Of sweet-smelling fields,
of spring grass after rain,
of the opening buds of the
Rose of Sharon.
We worship the Holy Breath
Which is placed higher
Than all the other things created.
For, lo, the eternal and sovereign Luminous space,
Where rule the unnumbered stars,
Is the air we breathe in
And the air we breathe out.
And in the moment betwixt the breathing in
And the breathing out
Is hidden all the mysteries of the Infinite Garden.*

Angel of Air,
Holy messenger of the Earthly Mother,
Enter deep within me,
As the swallow plummets from the sky,
That I may know the secrets of the wind
And the music of the stars.

The fourth Communion is with
The Angel of Earth,
She who brings forth corn and grapes
From the fullness of the earth,
She who brings children
From the loins of husband and wife.
He who would till the earth,
With the left arm and the right,
Unto him will she bring forth
An abundance of fruit and grain,
Golden-hued plants
Growing up from the earth
During the spring,
As far as the earth extends,
As far as the rivers stretch,
As far as the sun rises,
To impart their gifts of food unto men.
This wide earth do I praise,
Expanded far with paths,
The productive, the full-bearing,
Thy mother, holy plant!
Yea, I praise the lands
Where thou dost grow,
Sweet-scented, swiftly spreading,
The good growth of the Lord.
He who sows corn, grass, and fruit,

Soweth the Law.
And his harvest shall be bountiful,
And his crop shall be ripe upon the hills.
As a reward for the followers of the Law,
The Lord sent the Angel of Earth,
Holy messenger of the Earthly Mother,
To make the plants to grow,
And to make fertile the womb of woman,
That the earth may never be without
The laughter of children.
Let us worship the Lord in her!

The fifth Communion is with
The Angel of Life,
She who gives strength and vigor to man.
For, lo, if the wax is not pure,
How then can the candle give a steady flame?
Go, then, toward the high-growing trees,
And before one of them which is beautiful,
High-growing and mighty,
Say these words:
'Hail be unto thee! O good, living tree,
Made by the Creator!'
Then shall the River of Life
Flow between you and your Brother,
The Tree,
And health of the body,
Swiftness of foot,
Quick hearing of the ears,
Strength of the arms
And eyesight of the eagle be yours.
Such is the Communion

With the Angel of Life,
Holy messenger of the Earthly Mother.

The sixth Communion is with
The Angel of Joy,
She who descends upon earth
To give beauty to all men.
For the Lord is not worshipped with sadness,
Nor with cries of despair.
Leave off your moans and lamentations,
And sing unto the Lord a new song:
Sing unto the Lord, all the earth.
Let the heavens rejoice
And let the earth be glad.
Let the field be joyful,
Let the floods clap their hands;
Let the hills be joyful together
Before the Lord.
For you shall go out with joy
And be led forth with peace:
The mountains and the hills
Shall break forth before you into singing.
Angel of Joy,
Holy messenger of the Earthly Mother,
I will sing unto the Lord
As long as I live:
I will sing praise to my God
While I have my being.

The seventh Communion is with
Our Earthly Mother,
She who sends forth her Angels
To guide the roots of man
And send them deep into the blessed soil.

We invoke the Earthly Mother!
The Holy Preserver!
The Maintainer!
It is She who will restore the world!
The earth is hers,
And the fullness thereof: the world,
And they that dwell therein.
We worship the good, the strong,
The beneficent Earthly Mother
And all her Angels,
Bounteous, valiant,
And full of strength;
Welfare-bestowing, kind,
And health-giving.
Through her brightness and glory
Do the plants grow up from the earth,
By the never-failing springs.
Through her brightness and glory
Do the winds blow,
Driving down the clouds
Towards the never-failing springs.
The Earthly Mother and I are One.
I have my roots in her,
And she takes her delight in me
According to the Holy Law."

Then there was a great silence, as the listeners pondered the words of Jesus. And there was new strength in them, and desire and hope shone in their faces. And then one man spoke: "Master, we are filled with eagerness to begin our Communions with the Angels of the Earthly Mother, who planted the Great Garden of the Earth. But what of the Angels of the Heavenly Father, who rule the night? How are we to talk to them, who are so far above us, who are invisible to our eyes? For we can see the rays of the sun, we can feel the cool water of the stream where we bathe, and the grapes are warm to our touch as they grow purple on the vines. But the Angels of the Heavenly Father cannot be seen, or heard, or touched. How then can we talk to them, and enter their Infinite Garden? Master, tell us what we must do."

And the morning sun encircled his head with glory as Jesus looked upon them and spoke:

"My children, know you not that the Earth
And all that dwells therein
Is but a reflection of the
Kingdom of the Heavenly Father?
And as you are suckled and comforted
By your mother when a child,
But go to join your father in the fields
When you grow up,
So do the Angels of the Earthly Mother
Guide your steps
Toward him who is your Father,
And all his holy Angels,
That you may know your true home
And become true Sons of God.
While we are children,
We will see the rays of the sun,
But not the Power which created it;
While we are children,
We will hear the sounds of the flowing brook,
But not the Love which created it;
While we are children,
We will see the stars,
But not the hand which scatters them
Through the sky,

As the farmer scatters his seed.
Only through the Communions
With the Angels of the Heavenly Father,
Will we learn to see the unseen,
To hear that which cannot be heard,
And to speak the unspoken word.

The first Communion is with
The Angel of Power,
Who fills the sun with heat,
And guides the hand of man
In all his works.
Thine, O Heavenly Father!
Was the Power,
When thou didst order a path
For each of us and all.
Through thy power
Will my feet tread the
Path of the Law;
Through thy power
Will my hands perform thy works.
May the golden river of power
Always flow from thee to me,
And may my body always turn unto thee,
As the flower turns unto the sun.
For there is no power save that
From the Heavenly Father;
All else is but a dream of dust,
A cloud passing over the face of the sun.
There is no man that hath power
Over the spirit;
Neither hath he power in the day of death.
Only that power which cometh from God

Can carry us out from the City of Death.
Guide our works and deeds,
O Angel of Power,
Holy messenger of the Heavenly Father!

The second Communion is with
The Angel of Love,
Whose healing waters flow
In a never-ending stream
From the Sea of Eternity.
Beloved, let us love one another:
For love is of the Heavenly Father,
And everyone that loveth
Is born of the Heavenly Order
And knoweth the angels.
For without love,
A man's heart is parched and cracked
As the bottom of a dry well,
And his words are empty
As a hollow gourd.
But loving words are as a honeycomb
Sweet to the soul;
Loving words in a man's mouth
Are as deep waters,
And the wellspring of love
As a flowing brook.
Yea, it was said in the ancient of days,
Thou shalt love thy Heavenly Father
With all thy heart,
And with all thy mind,
And with all thy deeds,
And thou shalt love thy brothers
As thyself.

The Heavenly Father is love;
And he that dwelleth in love
Dwelleth in the Heavenly Father,
And the Heavenly Father in him.
He that loveth not is as a wandering bird
Cast out of the nest;
For him the grass faileth
And the stream has a bitter taste.
And if a man say,
I love the Heavenly Father
But hate my brother,
He is a liar:
For he that loveth not his brother
Whom he hath seen,
How can he love the Heavenly Father
Whom he hath not seen?
By this we know the Children of Light:
Those who walk with the Angel of Love,
For they love the Heavenly Father,
And they love their brethren,
And they keep the Holy Law.
Love is stronger
Than the currents of deep waters:
Love is stronger than death.

The third Communion is with
The Angel of Wisdom,
Who maketh man free from fear,
Wide of heart,
And easy of conscience:
Holy Wisdom,
The Understanding that unfolds,
Continuously,

As a holy scroll,
Yet does not come through learning.
All wisdom cometh
From the Heavenly Father,
And is with him forever.
Who can number the sand of the sea,
And the drops of rain,
And the days of eternity?
Who can find out the height of heaven,
And the breadth of the earth?
Who can tell the beginning
Of wisdom?
Wisdom hath been created
Before all things.
He who is without wisdom
Is like unto him that saith to the wood,
'Awake,' and to the dumb stone,
'Arise, and teach!'
So are his words empty,
And his deeds harmful,
As a child who brandishes his father's sword
And knoweth not its cutting edge.
But the crown of wisdom
Makes peace and perfect health
To flourish,
Both of which are the gifts of God.
O thou Heavenly Order!
And thou, Angel of Wisdom!
I will worship thee and
The Heavenly Father,
Because of whom
The river of thought within us

*Is flowing towards the
Holy Sea of Eternity.*

*The fourth Communion is with
The Angel of Eternal Life,
Who brings the message of eternity
To man.
For he who walks with the angels
Shall learn to soar
Above the clouds,
And his home shall be
In the Eternal Sea
Where stands the sacred Tree of Life.
Do not wait for death
To reveal the great mystery;
If you know not your Heavenly Father
While your feet tread the dusty soil,
There shall be naught but shadows for thee
In the life that is to come.
Here and now
Is the mystery revealed.
Here and now
Is the curtain lifted.
Be not afraid, O man!
Lay hold of the wings of the
Angel of Eternal Life,
And soar into the paths of the stars,
The moon, the sun,
And the endless Light,
Moving around in their
Revolving circle forever,
And fly toward the Heavenly Sea
Of Eternal Life.*

The fifth Communion is with
The Angel of Work,
Who sings in the humming of the bee,
Pausing not in its making of golden honey;
In the flute of the shepherd,
Who sleeps not lest his flock go astray;
In the song of the maiden
As she lays her hand to the spindle.
And if you think that these
Are not as fair in the eyes of the Lord
As the loftiest of prayers
Echoed from the highest mountain,
Then you do indeed err.
For the honest work of humble hands
Is a daily prayer of thanksgiving,
And the music of the plough
Is a joyful song unto the Lord.
He who eats the bread of idleness
must die of hunger,
For a field of stones
Can yield only stones.
For him is the day without meaning,
And the night a bitter journey of evil dreams.
The mind of the idle
Is full of the weeds of discontent;
But he who walks with the
Angel of Work
Has within him a field always fertile,
Where corn and grapes
And all manner of sweet-scented
Herbs and flowers grow in abundance.
As ye sow, so shall ye reap.

*The man of God who has found his task
Shall not ask any other blessing.*

*The sixth Communion is with
The Angel of Peace,
Whose kiss bestoweth calm,
And whose face is as the surface
Of untroubled waters,
Wherein the moon is reflected.
I will invoke Peace,
Whose breath is friendly,
Whose hand smooths the troubled brow.
In the reign of Peace,
There is neither hunger nor thirst,
Neither cold wind nor hot wind,
Neither old age nor death.
But to him that hath not peace in his soul,
There is no place to build within
The Holy Temple;
For how can the carpenter build
In the midst of a whirlwind?
The seed of violence can reap
Only a harvest of desolation,
And from the parched clay
Can grow no living thing.
Seek ye then the Angel of Peace,
Who is as the morning star
In the midst of a cloud,
As the moon at the full,
As a fair olive tree budding forth fruit,
And as the sun shining on the temple
Of the most High.*

Peace dwells in the heart of silence:
Be still, and know that I am God.

The seventh Communion is with
The Heavenly Father,
Who is,
Who was, and
Who ever shall be.
O Great Creator!
Thou didst create the Heavenly Angels,
And thou didst reveal the
Heavenly Laws!
Thou art my refuge and my fortress,
Thou art from everlasting.
Lord, thou hast been our dwelling place
In all generations.
Before the mountains were brought forth,
Or ever thou hast formed the earth,
Even from everlasting to everlasting,
Thou art God.
Who hath made the waters,
And who maketh the plants?
Who to the wind
Hath yoked the storm-clouds,
The swift and even the fleetest?
Who, O Great Creator!
Is the fountain of Eternal Life
Within our souls?
Who hath made the Light and the Darkness?
Who hath made sleep
And the zest of the waking hours?
Who spread the noontides
And the midnight?

Thou, O Great Creator!
Thou hast made the earth
By thy power,
Hath established the world
By thy wisdom,
And hath stretched out the heavens
By thy love.
Do thou reveal unto me,
O Heavenly Father,
Thy nature,
Which is the power of the
Angels of thy Holy Kingdom.
Immortality and the Heavenly Order
Hast thou given, O Creator,
And the best of all things,
Thy Holy Law!
I will praise thy works
With songs of thanksgiving,
Continually,
In all the generations of time.
With the coming of day,
I embrace my Mother.
With the coming of night,
I join my Father.
And with the outgoing
Of evening and morning,
I will breathe Their Law,
And I will not interrupt these Communions
Until the end of time "

And over heaven and earth was a great silence, and the peace of the Heavenly Father and the Earthly Mother shone over the heads of Jesus and the multitude.

FROM THE ESSENE BOOK OF JESUS

THE SEVENFOLD PEACE

And seeing the multitudes, Jesus went up into a mountain, and his disciples came unto him, and all those who hungered for his words. And seeing them gathered, he opened his mouth and taught them, saying:

"Peace I bring to thee, my children,
The Sevenfold Peace
Of the Earthly Mother
And the Heavenly Father.
Peace I bring to thy body,
Guided by the Angel of Power;
Peace I bring to thy heart,
Guided by the Angel of Love;
Peace I bring to thy mind,
Guided by the Angel of Wisdom.
Through the Angels of
Power, Love, and Wisdom,
Thou shalt travel the Seven Paths
Of the Infinite Garden,
And thy body, thy heart, and thy mind
Shall join in Oneness
In the Sacred Flight to the
Heavenly Sea of Peace.

Yea, I tell thee truly,
The paths are seven
Through the Infinite Garden,
And each must be traversed
By the body, the heart, and the mind

As one,
Lest thou stumble and fall
Into the abyss of emptiness.

For as a bird cannot fly with one wing,
So doth thy Bird of Wisdom
Need two wings of Power and Love
To soar above the abyss
To the Holy Tree of Life.

For the body alone
Is an abandoned house seen from afar:
What was thought beautiful
Is but ruin and desolation
When drawing near.
The body alone
Is as a chariot fashioned from gold,
Whose maker sets it on a pedestal,
Loath to soil it with use.
But as a golden idol,
It is ugly and without grace,
For only in movement
Doth it reveal its purpose.
Like the hollow blackness of a window
When the wind puts out its candle,
Is the body alone,
With no heart and no mind
To fill it with light.

And the heart alone
is a sun with no earth to shine upon,
A light in the void,
A ball of warmth drowned
In a sea of blackness.

For when a man doth love,
That love turneth only to
Its own destruction
When there is no hand to stretch forth

In good works,
And no mind to weave the flames of desire
Into a tapestry of psalms.
Like a whirlwind in the desert
Is the heart alone,
With no body and no mind
To lead it singing
Through the cypress and the pine.

And the mind alone
Is a holy scroll
Which has worn thin with the years,
And must be buried.
The truth and beauty of its words
Have not changed,
But the eyes can no longer read
The faded letters,
And it falleth to pieces in the hands.
So is the mind without the heart
To give it words,
And without the body
To do its deeds.
For what availeth wisdom
Without a heart to feel
And a tongue to give it voice?
Barren as the womb of an aged woman
Is the mind alone,
With no heart and no body
To fill it with life.

For, lo, I tell thee truly,
The body and the heart and the mind
Are as a chariot, and a horse, and a driver.
The chariot is the body,
Forged in strength to do the will
of the Heavenly Father
And the Earthly Mother.
The heart is the fiery steed,
Glorious and courageous,
Who carries the chariot bravely,
Whether the road be smooth,
Or whether stones and fallen trees
Lie in its path.
And the driver is the mind,
Holding the reins of wisdom,
Seeing from above what lieth
On the far horizon,
Charting the course of hooves and wheels.

Give ear, O ye heavens,
And I will speak;
And hear, O earth,
The words of my mouth.
My doctrine shall drop as the rain,
My speech shall distil as the dew,
As the small rain
Upon the tender herb,
And as the showers upon the grass.

Blessed is the Child of Light
Who is strong in body,
For he shall have oneness with the earth.
Thou shalt celebrate a daily feast
With all the gifts of the Angel of Earth:

The golden wheat and corn,
The purple grapes of autumn,
The ripe fruits of the trees,
The amber honey of the bees.
Thou shalt seek the fresh air
Of the forest and of the fields,
And there in the midst of them
Shalt thou find the Angel of Air.
Put off thy shoes and clothing
And suffer the Angel of Air
To embrace all thy body.
Then shalt thou breathe long and deeply,
That the Angel of Air
May be brought within thee.
Enter into the cool and flowing river
And suffer the Angel of Water
To embrace all thy body.
Cast thyself wholly into his enfolding arms,
And as often as thou movest the air with thy breath,
Move with thy body the water also.
Thou shalt seek the Angel of Sun,
And enter into that embrace
Which doth purify with holy flames.
And all these things are of the
Holy Law of the Earthly Mother,
She who did give thee birth.
He who hath found peace with the body
Hath built a holy temple
Wherein may dwell forever
The spirit of God.
Know this peace with thy mind,
Desire this peace with thy heart,
Fulfill this peace with thy body.

*Blessed is the Child of Light
Who is wise in mind,
For he shall create heaven.
The mind of the wise
Is a well-ploughed field,
Which giveth forth abundance and plenty.
For if thou showest a handful of seed
To a wise man,
He will see in his mind's eye
A field of golden wheat.
And if thou showest a handful of seed
To a fool,
He will see only that which is before him,
And call them worthless pebbles.
And as the field of the wise man
Giveth forth grain in abundance,
And the field of the fool
Is a harvest only of stones,
So it is with our thoughts.
As the sheaf of golden wheat
Lieth hidden within the tiny kernel,
So is the Kingdom of Heaven
Hidden within our thoughts.
If they be filled with the
Power, Love, and Wisdom
of the Angels of the Heavenly Father,
So they shall carry us
To the Heavenly Sea.
But if they be stained
With corruption, hatred, and ignorance,
They shall chain our feet
To pillars of pain and suffering.
No man can serve two masters;*

Neither can evil thoughts abide in a mind
Filled with the Light of the Law.
He who hath found peace with the mind
Hath learned to soar beyond
The Realm of the Angels.
Know this peace with thy mind,
Desire this peace with thy heart,
Fulfill this peace with thy body.

Blessed is the Child of Light
Who is pure in heart,
For he shall see God.
For as the Heavenly Father hath given thee
His holy spirit,
And thy Earthly Mother hath given thee
Her holy body,
So shall ye give love
To all thy brothers.
And thy true brothers are all those
Who do the will of thy Heavenly Father
And thy Earthly Mother.
Let thy love be as the sun
Which shines on all the creatures of the earth,
And does not favor one blade of grass
For another.
And this love shall flow as a fountain
From brother to brother,
And as it is spent,
So shall it be replenished.
For love is eternal.
Love is stronger
Than the currents of deep waters.
Love is stronger than death.

*And if a man hath not love,
He doth build a wall between him
And all the creatures of the earth,
And therein doth he dwell
In loneliness and pain.
Or he may become as an angry whirlpool
Which sucks into its depths
All that floats too near.
For the heart is a sea with mighty waves,
And love and wisdom must temper it,
As the warm sun breaks through the clouds
And quiets the restless sea.
He who hath found peace with his brothers
Hath entered the kingdom of Love,
And shall see God face to face.
Know this peace with thy mind,
Desire this peace with thy heart,
Fulfill this peace with thy body.*

*Blessed is the Child of Light
Who doth build on earth
The Kingdom of Heaven,
For he shall dwell in both worlds.
Thou shalt follow the Law
Of the Brotherhood,
Which saith that none shall have wealth,
And none shall be poor,
And all shall work together
In the garden of the Brotherhood.
Yet each shall follow his own path,
And each shall commune with his own heart.
For in the Infinite Garden
There are many and diverse flowers:*

Who shall say that one is best
Because its color is purple,
Or that one is favored
Because its stalk is long and slender?
Though the brothers
Be of different complexion,
Yet do they all toil
In the vineyard of the Earthly Mother,
And they all do lift their voices together
In praise of the Heavenly Father.
And together they break the holy bread,
And in silence share the holy meal
Of thanksgiving.
There shall be no peace among peoples
Till there be one garden of the Brotherhood
Over the earth.
For how can there be peace
When each man pursueth his own gain
And doth sell his soul into slavery?
Thou, Child of Light,
Do ye gather with thy brothers
And then go ye forth
To teach the ways of the Law
To those who would hear.
He who hath found peace
With the brotherhood of man
Hath made himself
The co-worker of God
Know this peace with thy mind,
Desire this peace with thy heart,
Fulfill this peace with thy body.

Blessed is the Child of Light

Who doth study the Book of the Law,
For he shall be as a candle
In the dark of night,
And an island of truth
In a sea of falsehood
For know ye, that the written word
Which cometh from God
Is a reflection of the Heavenly Sea,
Even as the bright stars
Reflect the face of heaven.
As the words of the Ancient Ones
Are etched with the hand of God
On the Holy Scrolls,
So is the Law engraved on the hearts
Of the faithful who do study them.
For it was said of old,
That in the beginning there were giants
In the earth,
And mighty men which were of old,
Men of renown.
And the Children of Light
Shall guard and preserve
Their written word,
Lest we become again as beasts,
And know not the Kingdom of the Angels.
Know ye, too,
That only through the written word
shalt thou find that Law
Which is unwritten,
As the spring which floweth from the ground
Hath a hidden source
In the secret depths beneath the earth.
The written Law

*Is the instrument by which
The unwritten Law is understood,
As the mute branch of a tree
Becomes a singing flute
In the hands of the shepherd.
Many there are
Who would stay in the tranquil
Valley of ignorance,
Where children play
And butterflies dance in the sun
For their short hour of life.*

*But none can tarry there long,
And ahead rise the somber
Mountains of learning.
Many there are
Who fear to cross,
And many there are
Who have fallen bruised and bleeding
From their steep and rugged slopes.
But faith is the guide
Over the gaping chasm,
And perseverance the foothold
In the jagged rocks.
Beyond the icy peaks of struggle
Lies the peace and beauty
Of the Infinite Garden of Knowledge,
Where the meaning of the Law
Is made known to the Children of Light.
Here in the center of its forest
Stands the Tree of Life,
Mystery of mysteries.
He who hath found peace*

With the teachings of the Ancients,
Through the light of the mind,
Through the light of nature,
And through the study of the Holy Word,
Hath entered the cloud-filled
Hall of the Ancients,
Where dwelleth the Holy Brotherhood,
of whom no man may speak.
Know this peace with thy mind,
Desire this peace with thy heart,
Fulfill this peace with thy body.

Blessed is the Child of Light
Who knoweth his Earthly Mother,
For she is the giver of life.
Know that thy Mother is in thee,
And thou art in her.
She bore thee
And she giveth thee life.
She it was who gaveth thee thy body,
And to her shalt thou one day
Give it back again.
Know that the blood which runs in thee
is born of the blood
Of thy Earthly Mother.
Her blood falls from the clouds,
Leaps up from the womb of the earth,
Babbles in the brooks of the mountains,
Flows wide in the rivers of the plains,
Sleeps in the lakes,
Rages mightily in the tempestuous seas.
Know that the air which thou dost breathe
Is born of the breath

*Of thy Earthly Mother.
Her breath is azure
In the heights of the heavens,
Soughs in the tops of the mountains,
Whispers in the leaves of the forest,
Billows over the cornfields,
Slumbers in the deep valleys,
Bums hot in the desert.
Know that the hardness of thy bones
Is born of the bones
Of thy Earthly Mother,
Of the rocks and of the stones.
Know that the tenderness of thy flesh
Is born of the flesh
Of thy Earthly Mother,
She whose flesh waxeth yellow and red
In the fruits of the trees.
The light of thy eyes,
The hearing of thy ears,
These are born
Of the colors and the sounds
Of thy Earthly Mother,
Which doth enclose thee about,
As the waves of the sea enclose a fish,
As the eddying air, a bird.
I tell thee in truth,
Man is the Son
Of the Earthly Mother,
And from her did the Son of Man
Receive his whole body,
Even as the body of the newborn babe
Is born of the womb of his mother.
I tell thee truly,*

Thou art one with the Earthly Mother;
She is in thee, and thou art in her.
Of her wert thou born,
In her dost thou live,
And to her shalt thou return again.
Keep, therefore, her laws,
For none can live long,
Neither be happy,
But he who honors his Earthly Mother
And keepeth her laws.
For thy breath is her breath,
Thy blood her blood,
Thy bone her bone,
Thy flesh her flesh,

Thy eyes and thy ears
Are her eyes and her ears.
He who hath found peace
With his Earthly Mother
Shall never know death.
Know this peace with thy mind,
Desire this peace with thy heart,
Fulfill this peace with thy body.

Blessed is the Child of Light
Who doth seek his Heavenly Father,
For he shall have eternal life.
He that dwelleth in the secret place
Of the Most High
Shall abide under the shadow
of the Almighty.
For he shall give his angels charge over thee,
To keep thee in all thy ways.
Know ye that the Lord hath been

*Our dwelling place
In all generations.
Before the mountains were brought forth,
Or ever he had formed
The earth and the world,
Even from everlasting to everlasting,
Hath there been love
Between the Heavenly Father
And his children.
And how shall this love be severed?
From the beginning
Until the ending of time
Doth the holy flame of love
Encircle the heads
Of the Heavenly Father
And the Children of Light:
How then shall this love be extinguished?
For not as a candle doth it burn,
Nor yet as a fire raging in the forest.
Lo, it burneth with the flame
Of Eternal Light,
And that flame cannot be consumed.
Ye that love thy Heavenly Father,
Do ye then his bidding:
Walk ye with his Holy Angels,
and find thy peace with his Holy Law.
For his Law is the entire Law:
Yea, it is the Law of laws.
Through his Law he hath made
The earth and the heavens to be one;
The mountains and the sea
Are his footstools.
With his hands he hath made us*

And fashioned us,
And he gaveth us understanding
That we may learn his Law.
He is covered with Light
As with a garment:
He stretcheth out the heavens
Like a curtain.
He maketh the clouds his chariot;
He walketh upon the wings of the wind.
He sendeth the springs into the valleys,
And his breath is in the mighty trees.
In his hand are the deep places of the earth:
The strength of the hills is his also.
The sea is his,
And his hands formed the dry land.
All the heavens declare the Glory of God,
And the firmament showeth his Law.
And to his children
Doth he bequeath his Kingdom,
To those who walk with his angels,
And find their peace with his Holy Law.
Wouldst thou know more my children?
How may we speak with our lips
That which cannot be spoken?
It is like a pomegranate eaten by a mute:
How then may he tell of its flavor?
If we say the Heavenly Father
Dwelleth within us,
Then are the heavens ashamed;
If we say he dwellest without us?
It is falsehood.
The eye which scanneth the far horizon
And the eye which seeth the hearts of men

He maketh as one eye.
He is not manifest,
He is not hidden.
He is not revealed,
Nor is he unrevealed.
My children, there are no words
To tell that which he is!
Only this do we know:
We are his children,
And he is our Father.
He is our God,
And we are the children of his pasture,
And the sheep of his hand.
He who hath found peace
With his Heavenly Father
Hath entered the sanctuary
Of the Holy Law,
And hath made a covenant with God
Which shall endure forever.
Know this peace with thy mind,
Desire this peace with thy heart,
Fulfill this peace with thy body.
Though heaven and earth may pass away,
Not one letter of the Holy Law
Shall change or pass away.
For in the beginning was the Law,
And the Law was with God,
And the Law was God.
May the Sevenfold Peace
Of the Heavenly Father
Be with thee always.

FRAGMENTS IDENTICAL WITH THE DEAD SEA SCROLLS.

And Enoch walked with God;
and he was not;
for God took him.

Essene Genesis 5:24

The Law was planted in the garden of the
Brotherhood
to enlighten the heart of man
and to make straight before him
all the ways of true righteousness,
an humble spirit, and even temper,
a freely compassionate nature,
and eternal goodness and understanding and insight,
and mighty wisdom which believes in all God's
works
and a confident trust in His many blessings,
and a spirit of knowledge in all things of the Great
Order,
loyal feelings toward all the children of truth,
a radiant purity which loathes everything impure,
a discretion regarding all the hidden things of truth
and secrets of inner knowledge.

from the Manual of Discipline of the Dead Sea Scrolls.

Thou hast made it known unto me,
thy deep, mysterious things.
All things exist by Thee
and there is none beside Thee.
By thy Law

thou hast directed my heart
that I set my steps straight forward
upon right paths
and walk where thy presence is.

  from the Book of Hymns VII of the Dead Sea Scrolls.

The Law was planted to reward the Children of Light
with healing and abundant peace,
with long life,
with fruitful seed of everlasting blessings,
with eternal joy
in immortality of eternal Life.

  from the Manual of Discipline of the Dead Sea Scrolls.

I thank thee, Heavenly Father,
because thou hast put me
at a source of running streams,
at a living spring in a land of drought,
watering an eternal garden of wonders,
the Tree of Life, Mystery of Mysteries,
growing everlasting branches for eternal planting
to sink their roots into the stream of life
from an eternal source.
And thou, Heavenly Father,
protect their fruits
with the Angels of the Day
and of the Night
and with flames of eternal Light burning every way.

  from the Thanksgiving Psalms of the Dead Sea Scrolls.

I am grateful, Heavenly Father,
for thou hast raised me to an eternal height
and I walk in the wonders of the plain.
Thou gavest me guidance
to reach Thine eternal company
from the depths of the earth.
Thou hast purified my body
to join the army of the Angels of the Earth
and my spirit to reach
the congregation of the Heavenly Angels.
Thou gavest man eternity
to praise at dawn and dusk
thy works and wonders
in joyful song.

    from the Thanksgiving Psalms of the Dead Sea Scrolls.

I will praise Thy works
with songs of Thanksgiving
continually, from period to period,
in the circuits of the day, and in its fixed order;
with the coming of light from its source,
and at the turn of evening and the outgoing of light,
at the outgoing of darkness and the coming in of day,
continually,
in all the generations of time.

    from the Thanksgiving Psalms of the Dead Sea Scrolls.

May He bless thee with every good,
May He keep thee from all evil
and illumine thy heart with the knowledge of life
and favor thee with eternal wisdom.

*And may He give his Sevenfold blessings upon thee
to everlasting Peace.*

    from the Manual of Discipline of the Dead Sea Scrolls.

*With the coming of day
I embrace my Mother.
With the coming of night
I join my Father.
And with the outgoing of evening and morning
I will breathe Their Law,
and I will not interrupt these Communions
until the end of time.*

    from the Manual of Discipline of the Dead Sea Scrolls.

*He assigned to man two spirits with which he
should walk.
They are the spirits of truth and a falsehood,
truth born out of the spring of Light,
falsehood from the well of darkness.
The dominion of all the children of truth
is in the hands of the Angels of Light
so that they walk in the ways of Light.
The spirits of truth and falsehood struggle within
the heart of man,
behaving with wisdom and folly.
And according as a man inherits truth,
so will he avoid darkness.
Blessings on all that have cast their lot with the Law,
that walk truthfully in all their ways.
May the Law bless them with all good
and keep them from all evil
and illumine their hearts with insight into the things*

of life and grace them with knowledge of things eternal.

from the Manual of Discipline of the Dead Sea Scrolls.

I have reached the inner vision
and through thy spirit in me
I have heard thy wondrous secret.
Through thy mystic insight
thou has caused a spring of knowledge
to well up within me,
a fountain of power,
pouring forth living waters,
a flood of love
and of all-embracing wisdom
like the splendor of eternal Light.

from the Book of Hymns of the Dead Sea Scrolls.

FROM THE ESSENE BOOK OF
THE TEACHER OF RIGHTEOUSNESS

And the Master took himself to the banks of a stream where the people were gathered, those who did hunger after his words. And he blessed them, and asked them whereof they were troubled. And one did speak: "Master, tell us what are those things we should hold of high value, and what are those things we should despise?"

And the Master answered, saying, "All the ills which men suffer are caused by those things without us; for what is within us can never make us suffer. A child dies, a fortune is lost, house and fields burn, and all men are helpless, and they cry out, 'What shall I do now? What shall now befall me? Will this thing come to pass?' All these are the words of those who grieve and rejoice over events which do befall them, events which are not of their doing. But if we do mourn over that which is not in our power, we are as the little child who weeps when the sun leaves the sky. It was said of old, thou shalt not covet anything that is thy neighbor's; and now I say unto thee, thou shalt not desire anything which is not in thy power, for only that which is within thee doth belong to thee; and that which is without thee doth belong to another. In this doth happiness lie: to know what is thine, and what is not thine. If thou wouldst have eternal life, hold fast to the eternity within thee, and grasp not at the shadows of the world of men, which hold the seeds of death."

"Is not all that happens without thee, outside of thy power? It is. And thy knowledge of good and evil, is it not within thee? It is. Is it not, then, in thy power, to treat of all which doth come to pass in the light of wisdom and love, instead of sadness and despair? It is. Can any man hinder thee from doing thus? No man can. Then shalt thou not cry out, 'What shall I do? What shall now befall me? Will this thing come to pass?' For whatsoever may come to pass, thou shalt judge it in the light of wisdom and love, and see all things with the eyes of the angels."

"For to weigh thy happiness according to that which may befall thee, is to live as a slave. And to live according to the angels which speak within thee, is to be free. Thou shalt live in freedom as a true son of God, and bow thy head only to the commandments of the Holy Law. In this way shalt thou live, that when the Angel of Death cometh for thee, thou canst stretch out thy hands to God, and say, 'The Communions I have received from thee for knowing thy Law and walking in the paths of the angels, I have not neglected: I have not dishonored thee by my acts: see how I have used the eye which seeth within: have I ever blamed thee? Have I cried out against that which hath befallen me, or desired that it be otherwise? Have I desired to transgress thy Law? That thou hast given me life, I thank thee for what thou hast given me: so long as I have used the things which are thine, I am content: take them back and place them wherever thou mayest choose, for thine are all things, even unto eternity.'"

"Know ye, that no man can serve two masters. Thou canst not wish to have the world's riches, and have also the Kingdom of Heaven. Thou canst not wish to own lands and wield power over men, and have also the Kingdom of Heaven. Wealth, lands, and power, these things belong to no man, for they are of the world. But the Kingdom of Heaven is thine forever, for it is within thee. And if thou dost desire and seek after that which doth not belong to thee, then shalt thou surely lose that which is thine. Know ye, for I tell thee truly, that nothing is given nor is it had for nothing. For every thing in the world of men and angels, there is a price. He who would gather wealth and riches must run about, kiss the hands of those he admires not, waste himself with fatigue at other men's doors, say and do many false things, give gifts of gold and silver and sweet oils; all this and more must a man do to gather wealth and favor. And when thou hast achieved it, what then dost thou have? Will this wealth and power secure for thee freedom from fear, a mind at peace, a day spent in the company of the Angels of the Earthly Mother, a night spent in communion with the Angels of the Heavenly Father? Dost thou expect to have for nothing, things so great? When a man hath two masters, either he will hate the one, and love the other; or else he will hold to the one, and despise the other. Ye cannot serve God and also serve the world. Perchance thy well goeth dry, precious oil is spilled, thy house burneth, thy crops wither: but thou dost treat what may befall thee with wisdom and love. Rains again shall fill the well, houses can again be built, new seeds can be sown: all these things shall pass away, and come again, and yet again pass away. But the Kingdom of Heaven is eternal, and shall not pass away. Do ye not, then, barter that which is eternal, for that which dieth in an hour."

When men shall ask of thee, to what country dost thou belong, say ye not that thou art of this country or that, for of truth, it is only the poor body which is born in one small corner of this earth. But thou, O Child of Light, belongeth to the Brotherhood which doth encompass all the heavens and beyond, and from thy Heavenly Father hath descended the seeds not only of thy father and grandfather, but of all beings which are generated on the earth. In truth, thou art a son of God, and all men thy brothers: and to have God for thy maker and thy father and guardian, shall not this release us from all sorrow and fear?

Therefore, I say unto thee, take no thought to store up worldly goods, possessions, gold and silver, for these bring only corruption and death. For the greater thy hoard of wealth, the thicker shall be the walls of thy tomb. Open wide the windows of thy soul, and breathe the fresh air of a free man! Why take ye thought for raiment? Consider the lilies of the field, how they grow: they toil not, neither do they spin: and yet I say unto thee, that even Solomon in his glory was not arrayed like one of these. Why take ye thought for nourishment? Consider the gifts of thy Earthly Mother: the ripe fruits of her trees, and the golden grain of her soil. Why take ye thought for house and lands? A man cannot sell to thee that which he doth not own, and he cannot own that which already doth belong to all. This wide earth is thine, and all men are thy brothers. The Angels of the Earthly Mother walk with thee by day, and the Angels of the Heavenly Father guide thee by night, and within thee is the Holy Law. It is not meet for the son of a king to covet a bauble in the gutter. Take thy place, then, at the table of the celebration, and fulfill thy inheritance with honor. For in God we live, and move, and have our being. In truth, we are his sons, and he is our Father.

He only is free who liveth as he doth desire to live; who is not hindered in his acts, and whose desires attaineth their ends. He who is not restrained is free, but he who can be restrained or hindered, that man is surely a slave. But who is not a slave? That man only who desireth nothing which doth belong to others. And what are those things which belong to thee? My children, only the Kingdom of Heaven within thee, where the Law of thy Heavenly Father doth dwell, doth belong to thee. The Kingdom of Heaven is like unto a merchant man, seeking goodly pearls: who, when he had found one pearl of great price, went and sold all that he had, and bought it. And if this one precious pearl be thine forever, why dost thou barter it for pebbles and stones? Know ye, that thy house, thy land, thy sons and daughters, all the joys of fortune and sorrows of tribulation, yea, even that opinion which others do hold of thee, all these things belong to thee not. And if ye then do lust after these things, and hold fast to them, and grieve and exult over them, then in truth thou art a slave, and in slavery wilt thou remain.

My children, let not the things which are not thine cleave unto thee! Let not the world grow unto thee, as the creeping vine groweth fast to the oak, so that thou dost suffer pain when it is torn from thee.

Naked earnest thou from thy mother's womb, and naked shalt thou return thither. The world giveth and the world taketh away. But no power in heaven or earth can take from thee the Holy Law which doth reside within thee. Thou mayest see thy parents slain, and from thy country mayest thou be driven. Then shalt thou go with cheerful heart to live in another, and look with pity on the slayer of thy parents, knowing that by the deed he doth slay himself. For thou knowest thy true parents, and thou livest secure in thy true country. For thy true parents are thy Heavenly Father and thy Earthly Mother, and thy true country is the Kingdom of Heaven. Death can never separate thee from thy true parents, and from thy true country there is no exile. And within thee, a rock which standeth against all storms, is the Holy Law, thy bulwark and thy salvation.

FRAGMENTS FROM THE ESSENE GOSPEL OF JOHN

In the beginning was the Law, and the Law was with God, and the Law was God. The same was in the beginning with God. All things were made by him; and without him was not anything made that was made. In him was life; and the life was the light of men. And the light shineth in the darkness; and the darkness comprehended it not.

From the far place in the desert came the Brothers, to bear witness of the Light, that all men through them might walk in the light of the Holy Law. For the true light doth illumine every man that cometh into the world, but the world knoweth it not. But as many do receive the Law, to them is given the power to become the Sons of God, and to enter the Eternal Sea where standeth the Tree of Life.

And Jesus taught them, saying, "Verily, verily, I say unto thee, except a man be born again, he cannot see the Kingdom of Heaven."

And one man said, "How can a man be born when he is old? Can he enter a second time into his mother's womb, and be born?"

And Jesus answered, "Verily, verily, I say unto thee, Except a man be born of the Earthly Mother and the Heavenly Father, and walk with the Angels of the Day and the Night, he cannot enter into the Eternal Kingdom. That which is born of the flesh is flesh; and that which is born of the Spirit is spirit. And the flesh of thy body is born of the Earthly Mother, and the spirit within thee is born of the Heavenly Father. The wind bloweth where it listeth, and thou hearest the sound thereof, but canst not tell whence it cometh. So it is with the Holy Law. All men hear it, but know it not, for from their first breath it is with them. But he who is born again of the Heavenly Father and the Earthly Mother, he shall hear with new ears, and see with new eyes, and the flame of the Holy Law shall be kindled within him."

And one man asked, "How can these things be?"

Jesus answered and said unto him, "Verily, verily, I say unto thee, We speak that we do know, and testify that we have seen; and ye receive not our witness. For man is born to walk with the angels, but instead he doth search for jewels in the mud. To him hath the Heavenly Father bestowed his inheritance, that he should build the Kingdom of Heaven on earth, but man hath turned his back on his Father, and doth worship the world and its idols. And this is the condemnation, that light is come into the world, and men loved darkness, rather than light, because their deeds were evil. For everyone that doeth evil hateth the light, neither cometh to the light. For we are all Sons of God, and in us God is glorified. And the light which shineth around God and his children is the Light of the Holy Law. And he who hateth the light, doth deny his Father and his Mother, who have given him birth."

And one man asked, "Master, how can we know the light?"

And Jesus answered, "Verily, verily, I give unto thee a new commandment: that ye love one another, even as they love thee who work together in the Garden of Brotherhood. By this shall all men know that ye too are brothers, even as we all are Sons of God."

And one man said, "All thy talk is of the Brotherhood, yet we cannot all be of the Brotherhood. Yet we would worship light and shun darkness, for none there is among us who desireth evil."

And Jesus answered, "Let not thy heart be troubled: ye believe in God. Know ye that in our Father's house are many mansions, and our Brotherhood is but a dark glass reflecting the Heavenly Brotherhood unto which all creatures of heaven and earth do belong. The Brotherhood is the vine, and our Heavenly Father is the husbandman. Every branch in us that beareth not fruit, he taketh away: and every branch that beareth fruit, he purgeth it, that it may bring forth more fruit. Abide in us, and we in thee. As the branch cannot bear fruit of itself, except it abide in the vine, no more can ye, except ye abide in the Holy Law, which is the rock upon which our Brotherhood stands. He that abideth in the Law, the same bringeth forth much fruit: for without the Law ye can do nothing. If a man abide not in the Law, he is cast forth as a branch, and is withered; and men gather them, and cast them into the fire, and they are burned.

"And as the brothers abide in the love one for another, as the Angel of Love doth teach them, so we do ask that ye love one another. Greater love hath no man than this, to teach the Holy Law one to another, and to love each other as oneself. The Heavenly Father is in us, and we are in him, and we do reach out our hands in love and ask that ye be one in us. The glory which he gavest us we do give to thee: that thou mayest be one, even as we are one. For thy Father in Heaven hath loved thee before the foundation of the world."

And in this manner did the Brothers teach the Holy Law to them who would hear it, and it is said they did marvelous things, and healed the sick and afflicted with diverse grasses and wondrous uses of sun and water. And there are also many other things they did, the which, if they should be written everyone, even the world itself could not contain the books that should be written. Amen.

FRAGMENTS FROM

THE ESSENE BOOK OF REVELATIONS

Behold, the Angel of Air shall bring him,
And every eye shall see him,
And the Brotherhood,
All the vast brotherhood of the earth
Shall raise their voice as one and sing,
Because of him.
Even so, Amen.

I am Alpha and Omega, the beginning and the end;
Which is, which was, and which is to come.

And the voice spoke, and I turned to see
The voice that spoke with me.
And being turned, I saw seven golden candles;
And in the midst of their blazing light
I saw one like unto the Son of Man,
Clothed in white, white as the snow.
And his voice filled the air with the sound of rushing water;
And in his hands were seven stars,
Full of the flaming light of the heavens from whence they came.
And when he spoke, his face was streaming light,
Blazing and golden like a thousand suns.

And he said, "Fear not, I am the first and the last;
I am the beginning and the end.
Write the things which thou hast seen,
And the things which are, and the things which shall be hereafter;
The mystery of the seven stars which fill my hands,
And the seven golden candles, blazing with eternal light.

The seven stars are the Angels of the Heavenly Father,
And the seven candles are the Angels of the Earthly Mother.

And the spirit of man is the flame
Which streams between the starlight and the glowing candle:
A bridge of holy light between heaven and earth.

These things saith he that holdeth seven stars in his hands,
Who walketh in the midst of the flames of seven golden candles.
He that hath an ear, let him hear what the Spirit saith:
"To him that overcometh will I give to eat of the Tree of Life,
That standeth in the midst of the shining Paradise of God."

And then I looked, and, behold,
A door was opened in heaven:
And a voice which sounded from all sides, like a trumpet,
Spoke to me: "Come up hither,
And I will show thee things which must be hereafter."

And immediately I was there, in spirit,
At the threshold of the open door.
And I entered through the open door
Into a sea of blazing light.
And in the midst of the blinding ocean of radiance was a throne;
And on the throne sat one whose face was hidden.
And there was a rainbow round about the throne,
In sight like unto an emerald.
And round about the throne were thirteen seats:
And upon the seats I saw thirteen elders sitting,
Clothed in white raiment;
And their faces were hidden by swirling clouds of light.
And seven lamps of fire burned before the throne,
The fire of the Earthly Mother.
And seven stars of heaven shone before the throne,
The fire of the Heavenly Father.

And before the throne
There was a sea of glass like unto crystal:
And reflected therein
Were all the mountains and valleys and oceans of the earth,
And all the creatures abiding therein.
And the thirteen elders bowed down before the splendor of him
Who sat on the throne, whose face was hidden,
And rivers of light streamed from their hands, one to the other,
And they cried, "Holy, holy, holy,
Lord God Almighty,
Which was, and is, and is to come.
Thou art worthy, O Lord,
To receive glory and honor and power:
For thou hast created all things."

And then I saw in the right hand
Of him that sat on the throne,
Whose face was hidden,
A book written within, and on the backside,
Sealed with seven seals.
And I saw an angel proclaiming with a loud voice,
"Who is worthy to open the book,
And to loose the seals thereof?"

And no being in heaven, nor in earth, neither under the earth,
Was able to open the book, neither to look thereon.
And I wept, because the book could not be opened,
Nor was I able to read what there was written.
And one of the elders saith unto me, "Weep not.
Reach out thy hand, and take the book,
Yea, even the book with the seven seals, and open it.
For it was written for thee,
Who art at once the lowest of the low,
And the highest of the high."

And I reached out my hand and touched the book.
And, behold, the cover lifted,
And my hands touched the golden pages,
And my eyes beheld the mystery of the seven seals.

And I beheld, and I heard the voice of many angels
Round about the throne,
And the number of them was ten thousand times ten thousand,
And thousands of thousands, saying with a loud voice,
"All glory, and wisdom, and strength,
And power forever and ever,
To him who shall reveal the Mystery of Mysteries."
And I saw the swirling clouds of golden light
Stretching like a fiery bridge between my hands,
And the hands of the thirteen elders,
And the feet of him who sat on the throne,
Whose face was hidden.

And I opened the first seal.
And I saw and beheld the Angel of Air.
And between her lips flowed the breath of life,
And she knelt over the earth
And gave to man the winds of Wisdom.
And man breathed in.
And when he breathed out, the sky darkened,
And the sweet air became foul and fetid,
And clouds of evil smoke hung low over all the earth.
And I turned my face away in shame.

And I opened the second seal.
And I saw and beheld the Angel of Water.
And between her lips flowed the water of life,
And she knelt over the earth
And gave to man an ocean of Love.

And man entered the clear and shining waters.
And when he touched the water, the clear streams darkened,
And the crystal waters became thick with slime,
And the fish lay gasping in the foul blackness,
And all creatures died of thirst.
And I turned my face away in shame.

And I opened the third seal.
And I saw and beheld the Angel of Sun.
And between her lips flowed the light of life,
And she knelt over the earth
And gave to man the fires of Power.
And the strength of the sun entered the heart of man,
And he took the power, and made with it a false sun,
And, lo, he spread the fires of destruction,
Burning the forests, laying waste the green valleys,
Leaving only charred bones of his brothers.
And I turned my face away in shame.

And I opened the fourth seal.
And I saw and beheld the Angel of joy.
And between her lips flowed the music of life,
And she knelt over the earth
And gave to man the song of Peace.
And peace and joy like music
Flowed through the soul of man.
But he heard only the harsh discord of sadness and discontent,
And he lifted up his sword
And cut off the hands of the peacemakers,
And lifted it up once again
And cut off the heads of the singers.
And I turned my face away in shame.

And I opened the fifth seal.
And I saw and beheld the Angel of Life.
And between her lips
Flowed the holy alliance between God and Man,
And she knelt over the earth
And gave to man the gift of Creation.
And man created a sickle of iron in the shape of a serpent,
And the harvest he reaped was hunger and death.
And I turned my face away in shame.

And I opened the sixth seal.
And I saw and beheld the Angel of Earth.
And between her lips flowed the river of Eternal Life,
And she knelt over the earth
And gave to man the secret of eternity,
And told him to open his eyes
And behold the mysterious Tree of Life in the Endless Sea.
But man lifted his hand and put out his own eyes,
And said there was no eternity.
And I turned my face away in shame.

And I opened the seventh seal.
And I saw and beheld the Angel of the Earthly Mother.
And she brought with her a message of blazing light
From the throne of the Heavenly Father.
And this message was for the ears of man alone,
He who walks between earth and heaven.
And into the ear of man was whispered the message.
And he did not hear.
But I did not turn away my face in shame.
Lo, I reached forth my hand to the wings of the angel,
And I turned my voice to heaven, saying,
"Tell me the message. For I would eat of the fruit
Of the Tree of Life that grows in the Sea of Eternity."

And the angel looked upon me with great sadness,
And there was silence in heaven.
And then I heard a voice, which was like unto the voice
Which sounded like a trumpet, saying,
"O Man, wouldst thou look upon the evil thou hast wrought,
When thou didst turn thy face away from the throne of God,
When thou didst not make use of the gifts
Of the seven Angels of the Earthly Mother
And the seven Angels of the Heavenly Father?
And a terrible pain seized me as I felt within me
The souls of all those who had blinded themselves,
So as to see only their own desires of the flesh.
And I saw the seven angels which stood before God;
And to them were given seven trumpets.
And another angel came and stood at the altar,
Having a golden censer;
And there was given unto him much incense,
That he should offer it with the prayers of all the angels
Upon the golden altar which was before the throne.
And the smoke of the incense ascended up before God
Out of the angel's hand.
And the angel took the censer,
And filled it with the fire of the altar,
And cast it into the earth,
And there were voices and thunderings,
And lightnings, and earthquakes.
And the seven angels which had the seven trumpets
Prepared themselves to sound.

The first angel sounded,
And there followed hail and fire mingled with blood,
And they were cast upon the earth:
And the green forests and trees were burnt up,
And all green grass shriveled to cinders.

And the second angel sounded,
And as it were a great mountain burning with fire
Was cast into the sea:
And blood rose from the earth as a vapor.

And the third angel sounded,
And lo, there was a great earthquake;
And the sun became as black as sackcloth of hair,
And the moon became as blood.

And the fourth angel sounded,
And the stars of heaven fell onto the earth,
Even as a fig tree casteth her untimely figs,
When she is shaken of a mighty wind.

And the fifth angel sounded,
And the heaven departed as a scroll when it is rolled together.
And over the whole earth there was not one tree,
Nor one flower, nor one blade of grass.
And I stood on the earth,
And my feet sank into the soil, soft and thick with blood,
Stretching as far as the eye could see.
And over all the earth was silence.

And the sixth angel sounded.
And I saw a mighty being come down from heaven,
Clothed with a cloud:
And a rainbow was upon his head,
And his face was as it were the sun,
And his feet were pillars of fire.
And he had in his hand an open book:
And he set his right foot upon the sea, and his left on the earth,
And he cried with a loud voice, which was wondrous to hear:
"O Man, wouldst thou have this vision come to pass?"

*And I answered, "Thou knowest, O Holy One,
That I would do anything
That these terrible things might not come to pass."*

*And he spoke: "Man has created these powers of destruction.
He has wrought them from his own mind.
He has turned his face away
From the Angels of the Heavenly Father and the Earthly Mother,
And he has fashioned his own destruction."*

*And I spoke: "Then is there no hope, bright angel?"
And a blazing light streamed like a river from his hands
As he answered, "There is always hope,
O thou for whom heaven and earth were created."*

*And then the angel,
He who stood upon the sea and upon the earth,
Lifted up his hand to heaven,
And swore by him that liveth forever and ever,
Who created heaven, and the things that therein are,
And the earth, and the things that therein are,
And the sea, and the things which are therein,
That there should be time no longer:
But in the days of the voice of the seventh angel,
When he shall begin to sound,
The mystery of God should be revealed to those
Who have eaten from the Tree of Life
Which standeth forever in the Eternal Sea.
And the voice spoke again, saying:
"Go, and take the book which is open in the hand of the angel
Which standeth upon the sea and upon the earth."
And I went unto the angel, and said unto him,
"Give me the book,
For I would eat from the Tree of Life*

Which standeth in the middle of the Eternal Sea."
And the angel gave to me the book,
And I opened the book, and I read therein
What had always been, what was now,
And what would come to pass.

I saw the holocaust which would engulf the earth,
And the great destruction
Which would drown all her people in oceans of blood.
And I saw too the eternity of man
And the endless forgiveness of the Almighty.
The souls of men were as blank pages in the book,
Always ready for a new song to be there inscribed.

And I lifted up my face
To the seven Angels of the Earthly Mother
And the seven Angels of the Heavenly Father,
And I felt my feet touching the holy brow of the Earthly Mother,
And my fingers touching the holy feet of the Heavenly Father,
And I uttered a hymn of Thanksgiving:

> *I thank thee, Heavenly Father,*
> *Because thou hast put me at a source of running streams,*
> *At a living spring in a land of drought,*
> *Watering an eternal garden of wonders,*
> *The Tree of Life, Mystery of Mysteries,*
> *Growing everlasting branches for eternal planting*
> *To sink their roots into the stream of life*
> *From an eternal source.*
> *And thou, Heavenly Father,*
> *Protect their fruits*
> *With the Angels of the Day and of the Night*
> *And with flames of Eternal Light burning every way.*

*But again the voice spoke,
And again my eyes were drawn away
From the splendors of the realm of light.
"Heed thou, O Man!
Thou mayest step on the right path
And walk in the presence of the angels.
Thou mayest sing of the Earthly Mother by day
And of the Heavenly Father by night,
And through thy being may course the golden stream of the Law.
But wouldst thou leave thy brothers|
To plunge through the gaping chasm of blood,
As the pain-wracked earth shudders and groans
Under her chains of stone?
Canst thou drink of the cup of eternal life,
When thy brothers die of thirst?*

*And my heart was heavy with compassion,
And I looked, and lo,
There appeared a great wonder in heaven:
A woman clothed with the sun, and the moon under her feet,
And upon her head a crown of seven stars.
And I knew she was the source of running streams
|And the Mother of the Forests.*

*And I stood upon the sand of the sea,
And saw a beast rise up out of the sea,
And from his nostrils wafted foul and loathsome air,
And where he rose from the sea the clear waters turned to slime,
And his body was covered with black and steaming stone.
And the woman clothed with the sun
Reached out her arms to the beast,
And the beast drew near and embraced her.
And lo, her skin of pearl withered beneath his foul breath,*

And her back was broken by his arms of crushing rock,
And with tears of blood she sank into the pool of slime.
And from the mouth of the beast there poured armies of men,
Brandishing swords and fighting, one with the other.
And they fought with a terrible anger,
And they cut off their own limbs and clawed out their eyes,
Until they fell into the pit of slime,
Screaming in agony and pain.

And I stepped to the edge of the pool and
reached down my hand,
And I could see the swirling maelstrom of blood,
And the men therein, trapped like flies in a web.
And I spoke in a loud voice, saying,
"Brothers, drop thy swords and take hold of my hand.
Leave off this defiling and desecration of she
Who hath given thee birth,
And he who hath given thee thy inheritance.
For thy days of buying and selling are over,
And over, too, thy days of hunting and killing.
For he that leadeth into captivity shall go into captivity,
And he that killeth by the sword must be killed with the sword.
And the merchants of the earth shall weep and mourn,
For no man buyeth thy merchandise any more:
The merchants of gold, and silver, and precious stones,
And of pearls, and fine linen, and purple, and silk, and scarlet,
And marble and beasts, and sheep and horses,
And chariots and slaves and souls of men,
All these things can ye not buy and sell,
For all is buried in a sea of blood
Because thou hast turned thy back on thy father and mother,
And worshipped the beast who would build a paradise of stone.
Drop thy swords, my brothers, and take hold of my hand.

And as our fingers clasped,
I saw in the distance a great city,
White and shining on the far horizon, glowing alabaster.
And there were voices, and thunders, and lightnings,
And there was a great earthquake,
Such as was not since men were upon the earth,
So mighty an earthquake, and so great.
And the great city was divided into three parts,
And the cities of the nations fell:
And the great city came in remembrance before God,
To give unto her the cup of the wine
Of the fierceness of his wrath.
And every island fled away, and the mountains were not found.
And there fell upon men a great hail out of heaven,
Every stone about the weight of a talent.
And a mighty angel took up a stone like a great millstone,
And cast it into the sea, saying,
"Thus with violence shall the great city be thrown down,
And shall be found no more at all.
And the voice of harpers, and musicians, and of pipers,
And of singers, and trumpeters,
Shall be heard no more at all in thee;
And no craftsman, of whatsoever craft he be,
Shall be found any more in thee;
And the sound of a millstone shall be heard
No more at all in thee.
And the light of a candle shall shine
No more at all in thee;
And the voice of the bridegroom and of the bride shall be heard
No more at all in thee:
For thy merchants were the great men of the earth;
For by thy sorceries were all nations deceived.
And in her was found the blood of prophets, and of saints,

And of all that were slain upon the earth."

And my brothers laid hold of my hand,
And they struggled out of the pool of slime
And stood bewildered on the sea of sand,
And skies opened and washed their naked bodies with rain.
And I heard a voice from heaven, as the voice of many waters,
And as the voice of a great thunder:
And I heard the voice of harpers harping with their harps.
And they sung as it were a new song before the throne.

And I saw another angel fly in the midst of heaven,
Having the songs of day and night
And the everlasting gospel to preach unto them
That dwell on the earth,
Unto them that have climbed from the pit of slime
And stand naked and washed by the rain before the throne.
And the angel cried, "Fear God, and give glory to him;
For the hour of his judgment is come:
And worship him that made heaven, and earth,
And the sea, and the fountains of waters."

And I saw heaven open, and beheld a white horse;
And he that sat upon him was called Faithful and True,
And in Righteousness he doth judge.
His eyes were as a flame of fire,
And on his head were many crowns,
And he was cloaked in blazing light
And his feet were bare.
And his name is called the Word of God.
And the Holy Brotherhood followed him upon white horses,
Clothed in fine linen, white and clean.
And they entered the eternal Infinite Garden,

In whose midst stood the Tree of Life.
And the rain-washed naked throngs came before them,
Trembling to receive their judgment.
For their sins were many, and they had defiled the earth,
Yea, they had destroyed the creatures of the land and sea,
Poisoned the ground, fouled the air,
And buried alive the Mother who had given them birth.

But I saw not what befell them, for my vision changed,
And I saw a new heaven and a new earth:
For the first heaven and the first earth were passed away;
And there was no more sea.
And I saw the holy city of the Brotherhood
Coming down from God out of heaven,
Prepared as a bride adorned for her husband.
And I heard a great voice out of heaven saying,
"Lo, the mountain of the Lord's house
Is established in the top of the mountains
And is exalted above the hills;
And all people shall flow unto it.
Come ye, and let us go up to the mountain of the Lord,
To the house of God;
And he will teach us of his ways,
And we will walk in his paths:
For out of the Holy Brotherhood shall go forth the Law.
Behold, the tabernacle of God is with men,
And he will dwell with them, and they shall be his people,
And God himself shall be with them, and be their God.
And God shall wipe away all tears from their eyes;
And there shall be no more death,
Neither sorrow, nor crying,
Neither shall there be any more pain:
For the former things are passed away.

*Those who made war shall beat their swords into plowshares,
And their spears into pruninghooks:
Nation shall not lift up sword against nation,
Neither shall they learn war any more:
For the former things are passed away."*

*And he spoke again: "Behold, I make all things new.
I am Alpha and Omega, the beginning and the end.
I will give unto him that is athirst
Of the fountain of the water of life freely.
He that overcometh shall inherit all things,
And I will be his God, and he shall be my son.
But the fearful, and unbelieving,
And the abominable, and murderers, and all liars,
Shall dig their own pit which burneth with fire and brimstone."
And again my vision changed,*

*And I heard the voices of the Holy Brotherhood raised in song,
Saying, "Come ye, and let us walk in the light of the Law."
And I saw the holy city,
And the Brothers were streaming unto it.
And the city had no need of the sun,
Neither of the moon, to shine in it:
For the glory of God did lighten it.
And I saw the pure river of the Water of Life,
Clear as crystal, proceeding out of the throne of God.
And in the midst of the river stood the Tree of Life,
Which bore fourteen manner of fruits,
And yielded her fruit to those who would eat of it,
And the leaves of the tree were for the healing of the nations.
And there shall be no night there;
And they need no candle, neither light of the sun,
For the Lord God giveth them light:*

And they shall reign forever and ever.

>*I have reached the inner vision
And through thy spirit in me
I have heard thy wondrous secret.
Through thy mystic insight
Thou hast caused a spring of knowledge
To well up within me,
A fountain of power, pouring forth living waters;
A flood of love and of all-embracing wisdom
Like the splendor of Eternal Light.*

THE ESSENE GOSPEL OF PEACE
Book Three
Lost Scrolls of The Essene Brotherhood

Now we have proudly separated ourselves from Nature, and the spirit of Pan is dead. Men's souls are scattered beyond the hope of unity, and the sword of formal creeds sharply separates them everywhere. To live in harmony with the Universe made life the performance of a majestic ceremony; to live against it was to creep aside into a *cul de sac*. Yet, even now, whispers of change are stealing over the face of the world once more. Like another vast dream beginning, man's consciousness is slowly spreading outwards once again. Some voice from the long ago is divinely trumpeting across our little globe. To that voice, I dedicate this book.

E.B.S.

PREFACE

Book Three of the Essene Gospel of Peace

This third book of the Essene Gospel of Peace is a collection of texts of great spiritual, literary, philosophical, and poetical value, created by two powerful interwoven streams of tradition.

Chronologically, the first is the stream of traditions to which the Hebrew people were exposed in the Babylonian prison, dating from the *Gilgamesh* epics to the *Zend Avesta* of Zarathustra. The second is the stream of traditions flowing with poetical majesty through the Old and New Testaments, dating from the ageless Enoch and the other Patriarchs, through the Prophets and on to the mysterious Essene Brotherhood.

In the buried library of the Essene Brotherhood at the Dead Sea, where the greatest number of scrolls were found, the texts of these two streams of traditions were very much interwoven. They follow each other in a strange succession: the powerful cubistic simplicity of the first juxtaposed with the majestic expressionist poetry of the second.

The original texts of this collection may be classified into three approximate groups: about seventy percent of them are completely different from the ancient sacred books of the Avestas and the Old and New Testaments; twenty percent are similar, and ten percent are identical.

My desire in presenting this collection was to abstain from dry philological and exegetical interpretations, and instead to concentrate on their spiritual and poetical values, more attractive to twentieth century man. I tried to follow the style of my French translation of the first book of the Essene Gospel of Peace, which has now been published in seventeen languages, and has been distributed in over 200,000 copies.

I hope this Book Three will be as successful as Book One, and thus continue to bring these ageless inspirations to our disoriented century, guiding us, per *secula seculorum,* toward greater and greater light.

EDMOND BORDEAUX SZEKELY

INTRODUCTION

From the remote ages of antiquity, a remarkable teaching has existed which is universal in its application and ageless in its wisdom. Fragments of it are found in Sumerian hieroglyphs and on tiles and stones dating back some eight or ten thousand years. Some of the symbols, such as for the sun, moon, air, water, and other natural forces, are from an even earlier age preceding the cataclysm that ended the Pleistocene period. How many thousands of years previous to that the teaching existed is unknown.

To study and practice this teaching is to reawaken within the heart of every man an intuitive knowledge that can solve his individual problems and the problems of the world.

Traces of the teaching have appeared in almost every country and religion. Its fundamental principles were taught in ancient Persia, Egypt, India, Tibet, China, Palestine, Greece, and many other countries. But it has been transmitted in its most pure form by the Essenes, that mysterious brotherhood which lived during the last two or three centuries B.C. and the first century of the Christian era at the Dead Sea in Palestine and at Lake Mareotis in Egypt. In Palestine and Syria, the members of the brotherhood were known as Essenes and in Egypt as *Therapeutae*, or healers.

The esoteric part of their teaching is given in the Tree of Life, the Essene Communions with the angels, and the Sevenfold Peace, among others. The exoteric, or outer teaching, appears in Book One of *The Essene Gospel of Peace* and the recently discovered Dead Sea Scrolls.

The origin of the brotherhood is said to be unknown, and the derivation of the name is uncertain. Some believe it comes from

Esnoch, or Enoch, and claim him to be their founder, their Communions with the angelic world having first been given to him.

Others consider the name comes from Esrael, the elects of the people to whom Moses brought forth the Communions at Mount Sinai where they were revealed to him by the angelic world.

But whatever their origin, it is certain that the Essenes existed for a very long time as a brotherhood, perhaps under other names in other lands.

The teaching appears in the *Zend Avesta* of Zarathustra, who translated it into a way of life that was followed for thousands of years. It contains the fundamental concepts of Brahmanism, the Vedas and the Upanishads; and the Yoga systems of India sprang from the same source. Buddha later gave forth essentially the same basic ideas and his sacred Bodhi tree is correlated with the Essene Tree of Life. In Tibet the teaching once more found expression in the Tibetan Wheel of Life.

The Pythagoreans and Stoics in ancient Greece also followed the Essene principles and much of their way of life. The same teaching was an element of the Adonic culture of the Phoenicians, of the Alexandrian School of Philosophy in Egypt, and contributed greatly to many branches of Western culture, Freemasonry, Gnosticism, the Kabala, and Christianity. Jesus interpreted it in its most sublime and beautiful form in the seven Beatitudes of the Sermon on the Mount.

The Essenes lived on the shores of lakes and rivers, away from cities and towns, and practiced a communal way of life, sharing equally in everything. They were mainly agriculturists and arboriculturists, having a vast knowledge of crops, soil, and climatic conditions which enabled them to grow a remarkable variety of fruits and vegetables in comparatively desert areas and with a minimum of labor.

They had no servants or slaves and were said to have been the first people to condemn slavery both in theory and practice. There were no rich and no poor amongst them, both conditions being considered by them as deviations from the Law. They established their own economic system, based wholly on the Law, and showed that all man's food and material needs can be attained without struggle, through knowledge of the Law.

They spent much time in study both of ancient writings and special branches of learning, such as education, healing, and astronomy. They were said to be the heirs of Chaldean and Persian astronomy and the Egyptian arts of healing. They were adept in prophecy for which they prepared by prolonged fasting. In the use of plants and herbs for healing man and beast they were likewise proficient.

They lived a simple regular life, rising each day before sunrise to study and commune with the forces of nature, bathing in cold water as a ritual, and donning white garments. After their daily labor in the fields and vineyards they partook of their meals in silence, preceding and ending them with prayer. In their profound respect for all living things they never touched flesh foods, nor did they drink fermented liquids. Their evenings were devoted to study and communion with the heavenly forces.

Evening was the beginning of their day, and their Sabbath, or holy day, began on Friday evening, the first day of their week. This day was given to study, discussion, the entertaining of visitors, and the playing of certain musical instruments, relics of which have been discovered.

Their way of life enabled them to live to advanced ages of 120 years or more and they were said to have marvelous strength and endurance. In all their activities they expressed creative love.

They sent out healers and teachers from the brotherhoods, amongst whom were Elijah, John the Baptist, John the Beloved, and the great Essene Master, Jesus.

Membership in the brotherhood was attainable only after a probationary period of a year and three years of initiatory work, followed by seven more years before being admitted to the full inner teaching.

Records of the Essene way of life have come down to us from the writings of their contemporaries. Pliny the Roman naturalist, Philo the Alexandrian philosopher, Josephus the Roman historian, Solanius and others, spoke of them variously as "a race by themselves, more remarkable than any other in the world," "the oldest of the initiates, receiving their teaching from Central Asia," "teaching perpetuated through an immense space of ages," "constant and unalterable holiness."

Some of the outer teaching is preserved in Aramaic text in the Vatican in Rome. Some in Slavic text was found in the possession of the Habsburgs in Austria and said to have been brought out of Asia in the thirteenth century by Nestorian priests fleeing the hordes of Genghis Khan.

Echoes of the teaching exist today in many forms, in certain rituals of the Masonic order, in the symbol of the seven-branched candlestick, in the greeting "Peace be with you," used from the time of Moses, and even in the seven days of the week, which have long since lost their original spiritual meaning.

From its antiquity, its persistence through the ages, it is evident the teaching could not have been the concept of any individual or any people, but is the interpretation, by a succession of great Teachers, of the Law of the universe, the basic Law, eternal and unchanging as the stars in their courses, the same now as two or ten thousand years ago, and as applicable today as then.

The teaching explains the Law, shows how man's deviations from it are the cause of all his troubles, and gives the method by which he can find his way out of his dilemma.

Preface.. 143
Introduction.. 145
The Sevenfold Vow.. 153
The Essene Worship... 155

Texts From The Lost Essene Scrolls

The Angel of Sun... 157
The Angel of Water.. 161
The Angel of Air... 165
The Angel of Earth... 167
The Angel of Life... 171
The Angel of Joy.. 175
The Earthly Mother.. 179
The Angel of Power... 183
The Angel of Love... 187
The Angel of Wisdom.. 189
The Angel of Eternal Life..................................... 193
The Angel of Work...197
The Angel of Peace..201
The Heavenly Father..205
The Holy Law.. 211
The Angels...215
The Brotherhood..219
Trees..223
Stars...227
Moon..231
Psalms of Praise and Thanksgiving...................... 233
Laments... 239
Prophecies... 243

THE SEVENFOLD VOW

I want to and will do my best
To live like the Tree of Life,
Planted by the Great Masters Of our Brotherhood,
With my Heavenly Father,
Who planted the Eternal Garden of the Universe
And gave me my spirit;
With my Earthly Mother
Who planted the Great Garden of the Earth
And gave me my body;
With my brothers
Who are working in the Garden of our Brotherhood.

I want to and will do my best
To hold every morning my Communions
With the Angels of the Earthly Mother,
And every evening
With the Angels of the Heavenly Father,
As established by
The Great Masters Of our Brotherhood.

I want to and will do my best
To follow the Path of the Sevenfold Peace.

I want to and will do my best
To perfect my body which acts,
My body which feels,
And my body which thinks,
According to the Teachings
Of the Great Masters of our Brotherhood.

I will always and everywhere obey with reverence
My Master,

*Who gives me the Light
Of the Great Masters of all times.*

*I will submit to my Master
And accept his decision
On whatsoever differences or complaints I may have
Against any of my brothers
Working in the Garden of the Brotherhood;
And I shall never take any complaint against a brother
To the outside world.*

*I will always and everywhere keep secret
All the traditions of our Brotherhood
Which my Master will tell me;
And I will never reveal to anyone these secrets
Without the permission of my Master.
I will never claim as my own
The knowledge received from my Master
And I will always give credit to him
For all this knowledge.
I will never use the knowledge and power I have gained
Through initiation from my Master
For material or selfish purposes.*

*I enter the Eternal and Infinite Garden
with reverence to the Heavenly Father,
To the Earthly Mother,
And to the Great Masters,
Reverence to the Holy,
Pure and Saving Teaching,
Reverence to the Brotherhood of the Elect.*

THE ESSENE WORSHIP

PROLOGUE

When God saw that his people would perish
Because they did not see the Light of Life,
He chose the best of Israel,
So that they might make the Light of Life
To shine before the Sons of Men,
And those chosen were called Essenes,
Because they taught the ignorant
And healed the sick,
And they gathered on the eve of every seventh day
To rejoice with the angels.

WORSHIP

ELDER: Earthly Mother, give us the Food of Life!
BROTHERS: We will eat the Food of Life!
ELDER: Angel of Sun, give us the Fire of Life!
BROTHERS: We will perpetuate the Fire of Life!
ELDER: Angel of Water, give us the Water of Life!
BROTHERS: We will bathe in the Water of Life!
ELDER: Angel of Air give us the Breath of Life!
BROTHERS: We will breathe the Air of Life!
ELDER: Heavenly Father, Give us thy Power!
BROTHERS: We will build the Kingdom of God with the Power of the Heavenly Father!
ELDER: Heavenly Father, Give us thy Love!
BROTHERS: We will fill our hearts with the Love of the Heavenly Father!
ELDER: Heavenly Father, give us thy Wisdom!
BROTHERS: We will follow the Wisdom

of the Heavenly Father!
ELDER: Heavenly Father, give us Eternal Life!
BROTHERS: We will live like the Tree of Eternal Life!
ELDER: Peace be with thee!
BROTHERS: Peace be with thee!

THE ANGEL OF SUN

Up! Rise up and roll along!
Thou immortal, shining,
Swift-steeded Angel of Sun!
Above the Mountains!
Produce Light for the World!

Angel of Sun, thou art the Fountain of Light:
Thou dost Pierce the darkness.
Open thou the gate of the horizon!
The Angel of Sun doth dwell far above the earth,
Yet do her rays fill our days with life and warmth.
The chariot of the morning doth bring the light
Of the rising sun
And maketh glad the hearts of men.
The Angel of Sun doth illumine our path
With rays of splendor.
Angel of Sun!
Dart forth thy rays upon me!
Let them touch me; let them penetrate me!
I give myself to thee and thy embrace,
Blessed with the fire of life!
A molten flood of holy joy
Flows toward me from thee!
Onward to thee, Angel of Sun!
As no man can look upon the sun with naked eyes,
So no man can see God face to face,
Lest he be consumed by the flames
Which guard the Tree of Life.
Study, then, the Holy Law:
For the face of the Sun and the face of God
Can be seen only by the one who hath within him

The Revelation of the Law.
Thinkest thou that death is an end?
Thy thoughts are foolish as those of a child
Who sees dark sky and falling rain
And cries that there is no sun.
Wouldst thou grow strong in the Law?
Be, then, as the sun at noonday,
Which shineth with light and warmth on all men,
And giveth freely and abundantly of her golden glory.
Then shall the Fountain of Light flow back to thee,
As the Sun is never without light,
For it floweth freely, without restraint.
And when the Sun riseth,
Then the Earth, made by the Creator,
Becometh clean,
The running waters become pure,
The waters of the wells become pure,
The waters of the sea become pure,
The standing waters become pure,
All the Holy Creatures become pure.
It is through brightness and glory
That man is born who listens well
To the Holy Words of the Law,
Whom Wisdom holds dear.
Through their brightness and glory
Doth the Sun go his way,
Through their brightness and glory
Doth the Moon go her way,
Through their brightness and glory
Do the Stars go their way
unto the immortal, shining, swift-steeded Sun
Let there be invocation with sacrifice and prayer.
When the Light of the Sun waxeth brighter,

When the brightness of the Sun waxeth warmer,
Then do the heavenly forces arise.
They pour their Glory upon the Earth,
Made by the Heavenly Father,
For the increase of the Children of Light,
For the increase of the immortal,
Shining, swift-steeded Sun.
He who offers up a sacrifice
Unto the immortal, shining, swift-steeded Sun,
To withstand darkness,
To withstand death that creeps in unseen,
Offereth it up unto the Heavenly Father,
Offereth it up unto the angels,
Offereth it up unto his own soul.
He rejoiceth all the heavenly and earthly forces
Who offereth up a sacrifice
Unto the immortal, shining, swift-steeded Sun.
I will sacrifice unto that friendship,
The best of all friendships,
That reign between the Angel of Sun
And the sons of the Earthly Mother.
I bless the Glory and Light,
The Strength and the Vigor,
Of the immortal, shining, swift-steeded Angel of Sun!

THE ANGEL OF WATER

From the Heavenly Sea
the Waters run and flow forward
from the never-failing Springs.

To the dry and barren desert
Have the Brothers brought the Angel of Water:
That she might bring forth a garden and a green place,
Tree-filled and fragrant with flowers.
Cast thyself into the enfolding arms
Of the Angel of Water:
For she shall cast out from thee
All that is unclean and evil.
Let my love flow toward thee, Heavenly Father,
As the river flows to the sea.
And let thy love flow to me, Heavenly Father,
As the gentle rain doth kiss the earth.
As a river through the forest
Is the Holy Law.
All creatures depend on it,
And it denieth nothing to any being.
The Law is to the world of men
What a great river is to streams and brooks.
As rivers of water in a dry place
Are the Brothers who bringeth the Holy Law
To the world of men.
In water mayest thou drown,
And in water mayest thou quench thy thirst.
Thus is the Holy Law a two-edged sword:
By the Law mayest thou destroy thyself,
And by the Law mayest thou see God.
Heavenly Father!

*From thy Heavenly Sea flow all the Waters
That spread over all the seven Kingdoms.
This Heavenly Sea of thine alone
Goeth on bringing Waters
Both in summer and winter and in all seasons.
This Sea of thine purifteth the seed in males,
The womb in females,
The milk in female's breasts.
Thy Heavenly Sea floweth down unrestrained
Unto the big-seeded corn fields,
Unto the small-seeded pasture fields,
And unto the whole of the Earthly World.
A thousand pure Springs run toward the pastures
That give food to the Children of Light.
If any one shall sacrifice unto thee,
O thou holy Angel of Water!
To that one dost thou give both splendor and glory,
With health and with vigor of the body.
To him dost thou give a long enduring life,
And the Heavenly Sea, thereafter.
We worship all the holy waters
Which do quench the thirst of the earth,
All the holy waters that the Creator hath made,
And all the plants which the Creator hath made,
All of which are holy.
We do worship the Water of Life,
And all waters upon the earth,
Whether standing, or running, or waters of the well,
Or spring-waters which perennially flow,
Or the blessed drippings of the rains,
We do sacrifice unto the good and holy waters
Which the Law hath created.
Let the sea roar, and all the waters,*

The world, and they that dwell therein.
Let the floods clap their hands,
Let the hills be joyful together.
The voice of the Lord is upon the waters:
The God of Glory thundereth.
Heavenly Father! And thou, Angel of Water!
We are thankful to thee, and we bless thy name.
A flood of love welleth up
From the hidden places beneath the earth:
The Brotherhood is blessed forever
In the Holy Water of Life.

THE ANGEL OF AIR

We worship the Holy Breath
Which is placed higher than
All the other things created;
And we worship
The most true Wisdom.

In the midst of the fresh air of the forest and fields,
There shalt thou find the Angel of Air.
Patiently, she waits for thee
To quit the dank and crowded holes of the city.
Seek her, then, and quaff deeply
Of the healing draught which she doth offer thee.
Breathe long and deeply,
That the Angel of Air may be brought within you.
For the rhythm of thy breath is the key of knowledge
Which doth reveal the Holy Law.
The Angel of Air
Doth soar on invisible wings:
Yet thou must walk her unseen path
If thou wouldst see the face of God.
Sweeter than the finest nectar
Of honeyed pomegranate
Is the fragrance of the wind
In the grove of cypress.
Sweeter still the scent of the godly,
Who do revere and teach the Holy Law.
Holy is the Angel of Air,
Who doth cleanse all that is unclean
And giveth to all evil-smelling things a sweet odor.
Come on, come on, O clouds!
From above down on to the earth,

By thousands of drops,
Through their brightness and glory the winds blow,
Driving down the clouds
Toward the never-failing springs.
Vapors rise up from the vales of the mountains,
Nursed by the wind along the trail of the Law
Which increaseth the kingdom of Light.
The Heavenly Father hath made the earth by his power,
He hath established the world by his wisdom,
And hath stretched out the heavens by his will.
When he uttereth his voice,
There is a multitude of waters in the heavens,
And he causeth the vapors to ascend
From the ends of the earth;
He maketh lightnings with rain,
And bringeth forth the wind out of his breath.
As the sea is the gathering place of the waters,
Rising up and going down,
Up the aerial way and down on to the earth,
And up again the aerial way:
Thus, rise up and roll along!
And for whose rising and growing
The Heavenly Father
Hath made the eternal and sovereign luminous Space.
No man may come before the Face of God
Whom the Angel of Air letteth not pass.
Thy body must breathe the air of the Earthly Mother,
As thy spirit must breathe the Holy Law
Of the Heavenly Father.

THE ANGEL OF EARTH

We invoke the Abundant Earth!
That possesseth Health and Happiness
And is more powerful
Than all its Creatures.

This wide earth do we praise,
Expanded far with paths,
The productive, the full-bearing,
Thy mother, holy plant!
We praise the lands where thou dost grow,
Sweet-scented, swiftly spreading,
The good growth of the Earthly Mother.
We praise the good, the strong, the beneficent
Angel of Earth,
Who doth rejoice in the dew of heaven,
The fatness of the earth,
And the abundant harvest of corn and grapes.
We praise the high mountains,
Rich in pastures and in waters,
Upon which run the many streams and rivers.
We praise the holy plants of the Angel of Earth,
Which grow up from the ground,
To nourish animals and men,
To nourish the Children of Light.
The earth is the strong Preserver,
The holy Preserver, the Maintainer!
We praise the strength and vigor
Of the powerful Preserver, the earth,
Created by the Heavenly Father!
We praise the healers of the earth,
They who know the secrets of the herbs and plants;

To the healers hath the Angel of Earth
Revealed her ancient knowledge.
The Lord hath created medicines out of the earth,
And he that is wise shall use them.
Was not the water made sweet with wood,
That the virtue thereof might be known?
And to certain of the brothers he hath given skill,
That the Law might be honored and fulfilled.
With such do they heal men,
And taketh away their pains,
And of their works there is no end;
And from them is peace over all the earth.
Then give place to the healers, and honor them,
For the Heavenly Father hath created them:
Let them not go from thee, for thou hast need of them.
We praise the tillers of the soil,
Who work together in the Garden of the Brotherhood,
In the fields which the Lord hath blessed:
He who would till the earth,
With the left arm and with the right,
Unto him will she bring forth plenty of fruit,
And wholesome green plants and golden grain.
Sweetness and fatness will flow out from that land
And from those fields,
Along with health and healing,
With fullness and increase and plenty.
He who sows corn, grass, and fruit
Soweth the Holy Law:
He maketh the Law of the Creator to progress.
When all the earth shall be a garden,
Then shall all the bodily world become free
From old age and death, from corruption and rot,
Forever and forever.

Mercy and truth shall be met together,
Righteousness and peace shall kiss each other,
Truth shall spring out of the earth,
And glory shall dwell in our land.

THE ANGEL OF LIFE

Be not ungrateful to thy Creator,
for he hath given thee Life.

Seek not the Law in thy scriptures, for the Law is Life,
Whereas the scriptures are only words.
I tell thee truly,
Moses received not his laws from God in writing,
But through the living word.
The Law is living word of living God
To living prophets for living men.
In everything that is life is the Law written.
It is found in the grass, in the trees,
In the river, in the mountains, in the birds of heaven,
In the forest creatures and the fish of the sea;
But it is found chiefly in thyselves.
All living things are nearer to God
Than the scriptures which are without life.
God so made life and all living things
That they might by the ever-living word
Teach the laws of the Heavenly Father
And the Earthly Mother
To the Sons of Men.
God wrote not the laws in the pages of books,
But in thy heart and in thy spirit.
They are in thy breath, thy blood, thy bone;
In thy flesh, thine eyes, thine ears,
And in every little part of thy body.
They are present in the air, in the water,
In the earth, in the plants, in the sunbeams,
In the depths and in the heights.
They all speak to thee

*That thou mayest understand the tongue and the will
of the living God.
And scriptures are the works of man,
But life and all its hosts are the work of God.
First, O Great Creator!
Thou didst create the Heavenly Powers
And thou didst reveal the Heavenly Laws!
Thou gavest unto us understanding
From thine own mind,
And thou madst our bodily life.
We are grateful, Heavenly Father,
For all thy manifold gifts of life:
For the precious things of heaven, for the dew,
For the precious fruits brought forth by the sun,
For the precious things put forth by the moon,
For the great things of the ancient mountains,
For the precious things of the lasting hills,
And for the precious things of the earth.
We are grateful, Heavenly Father,
For the vigor of health, health of the body,
Wise, bright, and clear-eyed, with swiftness of foot,
Quick hearing of the ears, strength of the arms
And eyesight of the eagle.
For all the manifold gifts of Life,
We do worship the Fire of Life,
And the Holy Light of the Heavenly Order.
We do worship the Fire,
The good and the friendly,
The Fire of Life!
The most beneficial and the most helpful,
The Fire of Life!
The most supporting, the most bountiful,
That Fire which is the House of the Lord!*

*Behold now the Child of Light
Who doth commune with the Angel of Life:
Lo, now, his strength is in his loins,
And his force is in the muscles of his chest.
He moveth his legs like a cedar:
The sinews of his thighs are knit together.
His bones are as tubes of brass,
His limbs are like bars of iron.
He doth eat of the table of the Earthly Mother,
The grass of the field and the waters of the stream
Do nourish him;
Surely the mountains bring him forth food.
Blessed is his strength and beauty,
For he doth serve the Law.
A Sanctuary of the Holy Spirit
Is the body in which the Fire of Life
Doth burn with eternal Light.
We thank thee, Heavenly Father,
For thou hast put us at a source of running streams
At a living spring in a land of drought,
Watering an eternal garden of wonders,
The Tree of Life, Mystery of Mysteries,
Growing everlasting branches for eternal planting
To sink their roots into the stream of Life
From an eternal source.*

THE ANGEL OF JOY

The heavens smile, the earth celebrates,
the morning stars sing together,
and all the Children of Light shout for Joy.

O sing unto the Heavenly Father a new song:
Sing unto the Earthly Mother, all the earth.
Let the heavens rejoice, and let the earth be glad,
Let the sea roar, and the fullness of Eternal Life.
Let the field be joyful, and all that is therein:
Then shall all the trees of the wood
Rejoice before the Holy Law.
Sing unto the Heavenly Father,
All ye heavens of heavens,
And ye waters that be above the heavens,
All mountains and all hills,
Stormy wind fulfilling his word,
Fruitful trees and all cedars,
Beasts and all cattle,
Creeping things and flying fowl,
Kings of the earth and all people,
Princes and all judges of the earth:
Young men and maidens, old men and children,
Let them sing unto the Heavenly Father with Joy.
Sing unto the Lord with the harp, and voice of a psalm.
With trumpets and sound of pipes
Make a joyful noise before the angels.
Let the floods clap their hands:
Let the hills be joyful together before the Lord.
Make a joyful noise unto the Lord, all ye lands.
Serve the Heavenly Father and the Earthly Mother
With gladness and joy:

Come before their presence with singing.
The spirit of the Holy Law is upon me,
Because the Elders have anointed me
To preach good tidings unto the meek.
They have sent me to bind up the brokenhearted,
To proclaim liberty to the captives,
And the opening of the prison to them that are bound;
To comfort all that mourn,
To send unto them the holy Angel of Joy,
To give unto them beauty for ashes,
The oil of joy for mourning,
The garment of Light for the spirit of heaviness,
For weeping may endure for a night,
But joy cometh in the morning.
The people that walked in darkness
Shall see a great light,
And they that dwell in the land of the shadow of death,
Upon them shall shine the light of the Holy Law.
Drop down, ye heavens, from above,
And let the skies pour down happiness.
Let the people of sadness go out with joy,
And be led forth with peace:
Let the mountains and the hills
Break forth before them into singing,
That they might partake of the holy celebration,
And eat of the fruit of the Tree of Life,
Which standeth in the Eternal Sea
The sun shall be no more their light by day,
Neither for brightness
Shall the moon give light unto them:
But the Law shall be unto them an everlasting light,
And the Heavenly Father and the Earthly Mother
Shall be their eternal glory.

Their sun shall no more go down,
Neither shall their moon withdraw itself:
For the Law shall be their everlasting light,
And the days of their mourning shall be ended.
I will greatly rejoice in the Holy Law,
My soul shall be joyful in the angels;
For they have clothed me in garments of light,
They have covered me with robes of joy.
As the earth bringeth forth her bud,
And as the garden causeth its seeds to spring forth,
So the Heavenly Father will cause the Holy Law
To spring forth with gladness and joy
Before all the Children of Light.
In the Garden of the Brotherhood,
All the earth shines with holiness and abundant joy,
For there are the seeds of the Holy Law sown.
The Law is the best of all good
For the Children of Light:
It giveth unto them brightness and glory,
Health and strength of the body,
Long life in communion with the angels,
And eternal and unending joy.
We will sing unto the Heavenly Father,
And unto the Earthly Mother,
And unto all the angels,
As long as we live in the Garden of the Brotherhood:
We will sing praise unto the Holy Law
Forever and forever.

THE EARTHLY MOTHER

*Honor thy Earthly Mother,
that thy days may be long upon the land.*

*The Earthly Mother is in thee, and thou in her.
She bore thee; she giveth thee life.
It was she who gaveth thee thy body,
And to her shalt thou one day give it back again.
Happy art thou when thou comest to know her
And her kingdom.
If thou receivest thy Mother's angels
And if thou doest her laws,
Who doeth these things shall never see disease.
For the power of our Mother is above all.
She hath rule over all the bodies of men
And all living things.
The blood which runs in us
Is born of the blood of our Earthly Mother.
Her blood falls from the clouds,
Leaps up from the womb of the earth,
Babbles in the brooks of the mountains,
Flows wide in the rivers of the plains,
Sleeps in the lakes,
Rages mightily in the tempestuous seas.
The air which we breathe
Is born of the breath of our Earthly Mother.
Her breath is azure in the heights of the heavens,
Soughs in the tops of the mountains,
Whispers in the leaves of the forest,
Billows over the cornfields,
Slumbers in the deep valleys,
Burns hot in the desert.*

*The hardness of our bones
Is born of the bones of our Earthly Mother,
of the rocks and of the stones.
They stand naked to the heavens
On the tops of the mountains,
They are as giants that lie sleeping on the sides of the mountains,
As idols set in the desert,
And are hidden in the deepness of the earth.
The tenderness of our flesh
Is born of the flesh of our Earthly Mother,
Whose flesh waxeth yellow and red in the fruits of the trees,
And nurtures us in the furrows of the fields.
The light of our eyes,
The hearing of our ears,
Both are born of the colors and sounds
Of our Earthly Mother;
Which enclose us about
As the waves of the sea, a fish,
As the eddying air, a bird.
Man is the Son of the Earthly Mother,
And from her did the Son of Man
Receive his whole body,
Even as the body of the newborn babe
Is born of the womb of his mother.
Thou art one with the Earthly Mother;
She is in thee, and thou in her.
Of her wert thou born, in her dost thou live,
And to her shalt thou return again.
Keep, therefore, her laws,
For none can live long, neither be happy,
But he who honors his Earthly Mother
And doeth her laws.
For thy breath is her breath,*

Thy blood her blood,
Thy bone her bone,
Thy flesh her flesh,
Thy eyes and thy ears,
Are her eyes and her ears.
Our Earthly Mother!
Always are we embraced by her,
Always are we surrounded by her beauty.
Never can we part from her;
Never can we know her depths.
Ever doth she create new forms:
That which now existeth never was before.
That which did exist returneth not again.
In her kingdom all is ever new, and always old.
In her midst do we live, yet we know her not.
Continually doth she speak to us,
Yet never doth betray to us her secrets.
Ever do we till her soil and harvest her crops,
Yet we have no power over her.
Ever doth she build, ever doth she destroy,
and her work place is hidden from the eyes of men.

THE ANGEL OF POWER

Thine, O Heavenly Father!
was the Power, when thou didst order
a Path for each of us and all.

What is the Deed well done?
It is that done by the Children of Light
Who regard the Law as before all other things.
The best of all gifts, therefore,
Do I beseech of thee, O thou best of beings,
Heavenly Father!
That the Holy Law shall rule within us
Through thy Angel of Power!
I do approach thee with my invocations,
That thy great gifts of power
Will protect thy Heavenly Order,
And thy creative mind within us, forever.
We will extol thee, Heavenly Father,
O almighty king!
And we will bless thy power forever and ever.
So long as we be able and may have the power,
So long will we teach the people
Concerning these Deeds to be done by them
With faith toward the Heavenly Father,
The Earthly Mother, the holy Angels,
And all the Children of Light
Who till the soil of the Garden of the Brotherhood,
And in the desire for the coming of the Heavenly Orc
Into their souls and their bodies.
Thine, O Heavenly Father! Was the Power,
Yea, thine, O Creator of Love!

*Was the understanding and the spirit,
When thou didst order a path for each of us and all.
Through thy Power shall we go unto the people,
And teach them, saying, Trust in the Law,
And walk in the ways of the holy Angels,
So shalt thou dwell in the land,
And verily thou shalt be fed from the feast table
of the Earthly Mother.
Delight thyself also in the Power
of the Heavenly Father,
And he shall give thee the desires of thine heart.
Let not arrogancy come out of thy mouth:
For the Heavenly Father doth rule by the holy Law,
And by him actions are weighed.
He bringeth down to the grave, and bringeth up.
The Power of the Law maketh poor, and maketh rich:
His Power bringeth low, and lifteth up.
He raiseth up the poor out of the dust,
And lifteth up the beggar from the dunghill,
And maketh them inherit the throne of glory.
Out of heaven shall he thunder
Upon the children of darkness:
The Lord shall judge with Power the ends of the earth.
Hear the voices of the Brothers
Who cry out in the wilderness and barren desert:
Prepare ye the way of the Law,
Make straight the paths of the Heavenly Father,
And the Earthly Mother,
And all the holy Angels of the day and of the night.
Every valley shall be filled,
And every mountain and hill shall be brought low;
And the crooked shall be made straight,
And the rough ways shall be made smooth,*

And all flesh shall see the Power of the Law.
We extol thee, Heavenly Father,
For thou hast lifted us up.
O Lord, our Almighty Powerful Father,
We cried unto thee, and thou hast healed us.
From the grave thou hast brought up
The souls of the people;
Thou hast kept them alive,
That they should not go down to the pit.
O Heavenly Father, thou art the Law;
Early and late will we seek thy Angels:
Our souls thirsteth for the Law,
Our flesh longeth for the Law.
A river of holy Power is the Law
In a dry and thirsty land, where no water is.
Our lips shall praise thy Power while we live,
We will lift up our hands in thy name.
We will preserve, we will nurture thy Heavenly Order
Through the fulfillment of Deeds.
We will invoke and pronounce by day and by night
Thy holy Power,
And that Power shall come to help us;
It will be as if there were a thousand angels
Watching over one man.
Unto thee, Heavenly Father, belongeth all Power,
And also unto thee belongeth mercy:
For the holy Law doth render to every man
According to his work.

THE ANGEL OF LOVE

*Love is stronger
than the currents of deep waters.
Love is stronger than death.*

*Beloved, let us love one another:
For love is of the Heavenly Father:
And everyone that loveth is born
Of the Heavenly Father and the Earthly Mother,
And knoweth the angels.
Ye shall love one another,
As the Heavenly Father hath loved you.
For the Heavenly Father is love:
And he that dwelleth in love
Dwelleth in the Heavenly Father,
And the Heavenly Father in him.
Let him that love him be as the sun
When he goeth forth in his might.
Brothers, be ye all of one mind,
Having endless love and compassion one for another.
Thou shalt not avenge, nor bear any grudge
Against the children of thy people,
But thou shalt love thy neighbor as thyself.
If a man say,
I love the Heavenly Father, but hate my brother,
He is a liar:
For he that loveth not his brother whom he hath seen,
How can he love the Heavenly Father
Whom he hath not seen?
He who loveth the Heavenly Father
Loveth also his brother.*

Love ye also the stranger:
For ye were strangers in the land of Egypt.
It is said by the people,
Better a dinner of herbs where love is,
Than a stalled ox and hatred therewith.
Loving words are as an honeycomb,
Sweet to the soul, and health to the bones.
The words of a man's mouth are as deep waters,
And the wellspring of love as a flowing brook.
What doth the Law require of thee,
But to do justly, and to love mercy,
And to walk humbly with the angels.
By this do we know that the Angel of Love
Doth dwell in us,
When we love the Heavenly Father,
And keep his Law.
O Gracious Love!
O Creator of Love!
Reveal the best words
Through thy divine mind living within us.
Say to the Children of Light
Who till the soil in the Garden of the Brotherhood:
Honor all men.
Love the Brotherhood.
Obey the Law.

THE ANGEL OF WISDOM

To follow the Lord
Is the beginning of Wisdom:
And the knowledge
Of the Holy One
Is understanding.
For by him
Thy days shall be multiplied,
And the years of thy life
Shall be increased.

All Wisdom cometh from the Heavenly Father,
And is with him forever.
Through the holy Law doth the Angel of Wisdom
Guide the Children of Light.
Who can number the sand of the sea,
And the drops of rain, and the days of eternity?
Who can find out the height of heaven,
And the breadth of the earth,
And the deep, and wisdom?
Wisdom hath been created before all things.
One may heal with goodness,
One may heal with justice,
One may heal with herbs,
One may heal with the Wise Word.
Amongst all the remedies,
This one is the healing one
That heals with the Wise Word.
And one it is that will best drive away sickness
From the bodies of the faithful,
For Wisdom is the best healing of all remedies.

To follow the holy Law is the crown of Wisdom,
Making peace and perfect health to flourish,
Both which are the gifts of the angels.
We would draw near unto thee, O Heavenly Father!
With the help of thy Angel of Wisdom,
Who guides us by means of thy Heavenly Order,
And with the actions and the words
inspired by thy holy Wisdom!
Come to us, Heavenly Father, with thy creative mind,
And do thou, who bestoweth gifts
Through thy Heavenly Order,
Bestow alike the long-lasting gift of Wisdom
Upon the Children of Light,
That this life might be spent in holy service
in the Garden of the Brotherhood.
In the realm of thy good mind,
Incarnate in our minds,
The path of Wisdom doth flow
From the Heavenly Order,
Wherein doth dwell the sacred Tree of Life.
In what fashion is manifest thy Law,
O Heavenly Father!
The Heavenly Father makes answer:
By good thought
In perfect unity with Wisdom,
O Child of Light!
What is the word well spoken?
It is the blessing-bestowing word of Wisdom.
What is the thought well-thought?
It is that which the Child of Light thinketh,
The one who holdeth the Holy Thought
To be the most of value of all things else.
So shall the Child of Light grow

In concentration and communion,
And he may develop Wisdom,
And thus shall he continue
Until all the mysteries of the Infinite Garden

Where standeth the Tree of Life
Shall be revealed to him.
Then shall he say these victorious words:
O Heavenly Father!
Give unto me my task
For the building of thy Kingdom on earth,
Through good thoughts, good words, good deeds,
Which shall be for the Child of Light
His most precious gift.
O thou Heavenly Order!
And thou Universal Mind!
I will worship thee and the Heavenly Father,
Because of whom the creative mind within us
Is causing the Imperishable Kingdom to progress!
Holy Wisdom maketh all men free from fear,
Wide of heart, and easy of conscience.
Holy Wisdom, the understanding that unfolds forever,
Continually, without end,
And is not acquired through the holy scrolls.
It is ignorance that ruineth most people,
Both amongst those who have died,
And those who shall die.
When ignorance will be replaced by Holy Wisdom,
Then will sweetness and fatness come back again
To our land and to our fields,
With health and healing,
With fullness, and increase, and growth,

And abundance of corn and of grass,
And rivers of Peace shall flow through the desert.

THE ANGEL OF ETERNAL LIFE

*And Enoch walked with God;
and he was not; for God took him.*

*Upon the earth was no man created like Enoch,
For he was taken from the earth.
He was as the morning star in the midst of a cloud,
And as the moon at the full:
As the sun shining upon the temple of the most High,
And as the rainbow giving light in the bright clouds,
And as the flower of roses in the spring of the year,
As lilies by the rivers of waters,
And as the branches of the frankincense tree
In the time of summer,
And as a fair olive tree budding forth fruit,
And as a cypress tree which groweth up to the clouds.
The first follower of the Law was Enoch,
The first of the healers, of the wise,
The happy, the glorious, the strong,
Who drove back sickness and drove back death.
He did obtain a source of remedies
To withstand sickness and to withstand death;
To withstand pain and to withstand fever;
To withstand the evil and infection
Which ignorance of the Law
Had created against the bodies of mortals.
We invoke Enoch,
The master of life,
The Founder of our Brotherhood,
The man of the Law,
The wisest of all beings,*

The best ruling of all beings,
The brightest of all beings,
The most glorious of all beings,
The most worthy of invocations amongst all beings,
The most worthy of glorification amongst all beings,
Who first thought what is good,
Who first spoke what is good,
Who first did what is good.
Who was the first Priest,
The first Plougher of the Ground,
Who first knew and first taught the Word,
And the obedience to the Holy Law.
To all the Children of Light
He gave all the good things of life:
He was the first bearer of the Law.
It is written, the words of Father Enoch:
We sacrifice unto the Creator,
The Heavenly Father,
The bright and glorious Angels.
We sacrifice unto the shining heavens,
We sacrifice unto the bright, all-happy, blissful wisdom
Of the Holy Angels of Eternity.
Grant to us, Heavenly Father!
The desire and the knowledge of the straightest path,
The straightest because of the Heavenly Order of Life,
The best life of the angels,
Shining, all glorious.
As health is excellent, so also is Eternal Life,
Both flowing from the Heavenly Order,
The Creator of goodness of the mind,
And of actions of life performed for devotion
To the Creator of Eternal Life.
We sacrifice unto the sovereign sky,

We sacrifice unto the boundless time,
We sacrifice unto the endless sea of Eternal Life.
We do invoke the most glorious Law.
We invoke the Kingdom of Heaven,
The boundless time, and the angels.
We invoke the eternal, holy Law.
We follow the paths of the Stars,
The Moon, the Sun, and the endless Light,
Moving around in their revolving circle forever.
And truthfulness in Thought, Word, and Deed
Will place the soul of the faithful man
In the endless light of Eternal Life.
The Heavenly Father possessed me
In the beginning of his way, before his works of old.
I was set up from everlasting, from the beginning,
Or ever the earth was.
When there were no depths, I was brought forth:
While as yet he had not made the earth, nor the fields,
Nor the beginning of the dust of the world.
When he established the heavens, I was there:
When he set a circle upon the face of the deep:
When he made firm the skies above:
When the fountain of the deep became strong:
|When he gave to the sea its bound,
That the waters should not transgress his Law:
When he marked out the foundations of the earth:
Then I was by him, as a master workman:
And I was daily his delight,
Rejoicing always before him,
Rejoicing in his habitable earth,
And my delight was with the Sons of Men.
For eternity the Heavenly Father reigneth,
He is clothed with majesty and strength.

He is from everlasting!
The floods have lifted up, O Lord,
The floods have lifted up their voice,
The floods lift up their waves.
The Heavenly Father on high
Is mightier than the noise of many waters,
Yea, than the mighty waves of the sea.
His name shall endure forever,
His name shall be continued as long as eternity,
And all the Children of Light shall be blessed in him,
And all men shall call him blessed.
Let the whole earth be filled
With the glory of the Heavenly Father,
The Earthly Mother,
And all the holy Angels.
I have reached the inner vision
And through thy spirit in me,
I have heard thy wondrous secret.
Through thy mystic insight
Thou hast caused a spring of knowledge
To well up within me,
A fountain of power, pouring forth living waters,
A flood of love and of all-embracing wisdom
Like the splendor of Eternal Light.

THE ANGEL OF WORK

Who hath measured the waters
In the hollow of his hand,
And meted out heaven with a span,
And comprehended the dust of the earth
In a measure,
And weighed the mountains in scales,
And the hills in a balance?

The sun ariseth, and the Brothers gather together,
They go forth unto their work in the fields;
With strong backs and cheerful hearts they go forth
To labor together in the Garden of the Brotherhood.
They are the Workers of Good,
Because they work the good of the Heavenly Father.
They are the spirit, conscience, and soul of those
Who teach the Law and who struggle for the Law.
With the right arm and the left, they till the soil,
And the desert bursts forth in colors of green and gold.
With the right arm and the left, they lay the stones
Which shall build on earth the Kingdom of Heaven.
They are the messengers of the Angel of Work:
In them is revealed the holy Law.
O Heavenly Father! How manifold are thy works!
In wisdom hast thou made them all;
The earth is full of thy riches.
Thou sendest the springs into the valleys,
Which run among the hills.
Thou givest drink to every beast of the field,
And causeth the grass to grow for the cattle.
Thou settest the mighty trees in their places,
That the birds of heaven may have their habitation,

And sing sweetly among the branches.
Thou givest herbs for the service of man,
That he may bring forth food out of the earth.
In the hands of the Brothers all thy gifts bear fruit,
For they are building on earth the Kingdom of Heaven.
Thou openest thine hand; they are filled with good.
Thou sendest forth thy spirit; they are created,
And together with thy holy Angels,
They shall renew the face of the earth.
O thou Heavenly Father!
Thou who art one alone!
Reveal unto the Children of Light:
Which is the foremost place
Wherein the earth feeleth the greatest joy?
The Heavenly Father answering, said:
It is the place whereupon one of the Brothers,
Who follow the holy Law, steppeth forth:
With his good thoughts, good words, and good deeds!
Whose back is strong in service,
Whose hands are not idle,
Who lifteth up his voice in full accord with the Law.
That place is holy whereon one of the Brothers
Soweth the most of corn, of grass, of fruit:
Where he watereth that ground which is dry,
Or draineth the too-wet soil
For the earth hath been given unto the keeping
Of the Children of Light,
That they treasure and care for it,
And bring from its depths only that
Which is for the nourishment of the body.
Blessed are the Children of Light
Whose joy is in the work of the Law,
Who labor in the Garden of the Brotherhood by day,

And join the Angels of the Heavenly Father by night.
From their lips is the story told,
Which doth serve as a teaching for the Sons of Men:
It is said that the trees went forth on a time
To anoint a king over them;
And they said unto the olive tree,
"Reign thou over us."
But the olive tree said unto them,
"Should I leave my fatness,
Wherewith by me they honor God and man,
And go to be promoted over the trees?"
And the trees said to the fig tree,
"Come thou, and reign over us.
But the fig tree said unto them,
"Should I forsake my sweetness, and my good fruit,
And go to be promoted over the trees?"
Then said the trees unto the vine,
"Come thou, and reign over us.
And the vine said unto them,
"Should I leave my wine,
Which cheereth God and man,
And go to be promoted over the trees?"
The man of the Law who fulfills his tasks
Does not need further blessings.

THE ANGEL OF PEACE

For the earth shall be filled
with the Peace of the Heavenly Father,
as the waters cover the sea.

I will invoke the Angel of Peace,
Whose breath is friendly,
Whose hand is clothed in power.
In the reign of Peace, there is neither hunger nor thirst,
Neither cold wind nor hot wind,
Neither old age nor death.
In the reign of Peace,
Both animals and men shall be undying,
Waters and plants shall be undrying,
And the food of life shall be never-failing.
It is said that the mountains
Shall bring peace to the people,
And the little hills, righteousness.
There shall be peace
As long as the sun and moon endure,
Throughout all generations.
Peace shall come down like rain upon mown grass,
As showers that water the earth.
In the reign of Peace shall the Law grow strong,
And the Children of Light shall have dominion
From sea to sea, unto the ends of the earth.
The reign of Peace hath its source
In the Heavenly Father;
By his strength he setteth fast the mountains,
He maketh the outgoings of morning and evening
To rejoice in the Light,

He bringeth to earth the river of the Law,
To water and enrich it,
He maketh soft the earth with showers;
They drop upon the pastures of the wilderness,
And the little hills rejoice on every sidle.
The pastures are clothed with flocks;
The valleys also are covered over with corn;
They shout for joy, they also sing.
O Heavenly Father!
Bring unto thy earth the reign of Peace!
Then shall we remember the words
Of him who taught of old the Children of Light:
I give the peace of thy Earthly Mother
To thy body,
And the peace of thy Heavenly Father
To thy spirit.
And let the peace of both
Reign among the Sons of Men.
Come to me all that are weary,
And that suffer in strife and affliction!
For my peace will strengthen thee and comfort thee.
For my peace is exceeding full of joy.
Wherefore do I always greet thee after this manner:
Peace be with thee!
Do thou always, therefore, so greet one another,
That upon thy body may descend
The Peace of thy Earthly Mother,
And upon thy spirit
The Peace of thy Heavenly Father.
And then wilt thou find peace also among thyselves,
For the Kingdom of the Law is within thee.
And return to thy Brothers
And give thy peace to them also,

For happy are they that strive for peace,
For they will find the peace of the Heavenly Father.
And give to everyone thy peace,
Even as I have given my peace unto thee.
For my peace is of God.
Peace be with thee!

THE HEAVENLY FATHER

In the Heavenly Kingdom
There are strange and wondrous works,
For by his word all things consist.
There are yet hid greater things than these be,
For we have seen but a few of his works:
The Heavenly Father hath made all things.

The beauty of heaven, the glory of the stars,
Give light in the highest places of the Heavenly Sea.
Sentinels of the most High, they stand in their order,
And never faint in their watches.
Look upon the rainbow, and praise him that made it;
Very beautiful it is in the brightness thereof
It compasseth the heaven about with a glorious circle,
And the hands of the most High have bended it.
By his Law he maketh the snow to fall apace,
And sendeth swiftly the lightnings of his judgment.
Through this the treasures are opened,
And clouds fly forth as fowls.
By his great power he maketh the clouds firm,
And the hailstones are broken small.
At his sight the mountains are shaken,
And at his will the south wind bloweth.
The noise of the thunder maketh the earth to tremble:
So doth the northern storm and the whirlwind:
As birds flying, he scattereth the snow,
And the eye marvelleth
At the beauty of the whiteness thereof,
And the heart is astonished at the raining of it.
So do the heavens declare the glory of God,
And the firmament showeth his handiwork.

Who hath made the waters,
And who maketh the plants?
Who to the wind hath yoked the storm-clouds,
The swift and even the fleetest?
Who, O Heavenly Father,
Is the Creator of the holy Law within our souls?
Who hath made the light and the darkness?
Who hath made sleep and the zest of the waking hours?
Who gave the recurring sun and stars
Their undeviating way?
Who established that whereby the moon doth wax
And whereby she waneth?
Who, save thee, Heavenly Father,
Hath done these glorious things!
Lord, thou hast been our dwelling place
In all generations.
Before the mountains were brought forth,
Or ever thou hadst formed the earth and the world,
Even from everlasting to everlasting, thou art the Law.
Thy name is Understanding,
Thy name is Wisdom,
Thy name is the Most Beneficent,
Thy name is the Unconquerable One,
Thy name is He Who maketh the true account,
Thy name is the All-seeing One,
Thy name is the Healing One,
Thy name is the Creator.
Thou art the Keeper,
Thou art the Creator and the Maintainer;
Thou art the Discerner and the Spirit.
Thou art the Holy Law.
These names were pronounced
Before the Creation of this Heaven,

Before the making of the waters and of the plants,
Before the birth of our holy Father Enoch.
Before the beginning of time,
The Heavenly Father planted the holy Tree of Life,
Which standeth forever in the midst of the Eternal Sea.
High in its branches sings a bird,
And only those who have journeyed there,
And have heard the mysterious song of the bird,
Only those shall see the Heavenly Father.
They shall ask of him his name,
And he shall answer, I am that I am,
Being ever the same as the Eternal, I am.
O thou Heavenly Father!
How excellent is thy name in all the earth!
Thou hast set thy glory above the heavens.
When we consider thy heavens, the work of thy fingers,
The moon and the stars, which thou hast ordained,
What is man, that thou art mindful of him?
Yet thou hast made a covenant
With the Children of Light,
And they walk with thy holy Angels;
Thou hast crowned them with glory and honor,
Thou madest them to have dominion
Over the works of thy hands,
And gavest unto them
The task of nourishing and protecting
All that lives and grows on thy green earth.
O Heavenly Father!
How excellent is thy name in all the earth!
Hear the voice of one who cries out to thee:
Whither shall I go from thy spirit?
Or whither shall I flee from thy presence?
If I ascend up into heaven, thou art there;

If I make my bed in hell, behold, thou art there.
If I take the wings of the morning,
And dwell in the uttermost parts of the sea,
Even there shall thy hand lead me,
And thy right hand shall hold me.
If I say, "Surely the darkness shall cover me,
Even the night shall be light about me;
Yea, the darkness hideth not from thee
But the night shineth as the day:
The darkness and the light are both alike to thee,
For thou hast possessed my reins.
As the hart panteth after the water brooks,
So panteth my soul after thee, O God.
My soul thirsteth for the living Heavenly Father.
The Law is my light and salvation;
Whom shall I fear?
The Law is the rock and the strength of my life;
Of whom shall I be afraid?
One thing have I desired of the Law,
That I will seek after:
That I may dwell in the house of the Law
All the days of my life,
To behold the beauty of the Heavenly Father.
Those who dwell in the secret place of the most High
Shall abide under the shadow of the Almighty.
We will say of the Law,
"Thou art our refuge and our fortress;
We will trust in the Holy Law."
And the Heavenly Father
Shall cover us with his feathers,
And under his wings shall we trust;
His truth shall be our shield and buckler.
We shall not be afraid for the terror by night,

Nor for the arrow that flieth by day,
Nor for the pestilence that walketh in darkness,
Nor for the destruction that wasteth at noonday.
For by day we shall walk
With the Angels of the Earthly Mother,
By night we shall commune
With the Angels of the Heavenly Father,
And when the sun reacheth its zenith at noontide,
We shall stand silent before the Sevenfold Peace:
And no evil shall befall us,
Neither shall any plague come nigh our dwelling,
For he hath given his angels charge over us,
To keep us in all their ways.
The Heavenly Father is our refuge and strength.
Therefore will not we fear,
Though the earth be removed,
And though the mountains be carried
Into the midst of the sea,
Though the waters thereof roar and be troubled,
Though the mountains shake with the swelling thereof.
There is a river which floweth to the Eternal Sea.
Beside the river stands the holy Tree of Life.
There doth my Father dwell, and my home is in him.
The Heavenly Father and I are One.

THE HOLY LAW

Thou, O Holy Law,
The Tree of Life
That standeth in the middle
of the Eternal Sea,
That is called
The Tree of Healing.
The Tree of powerful Healing,
The Tree of all Healing,
And upon which rests the seeds
Of all we invoke.

Have ye-not known? Have ye not heard?
Hath it not been told thee from the beginning?
Lift up thine eyes on high, and behold the Holy Law,
Which was established before the eternal,
Sovereign and luminous space,
Which hath created the foundations of the earth,
Which is the first and the last,
Which liveth in the hearts of the Children of Light.
For the Law is great,
As the Heavenly Father is great above his angels:
He it is who giveth us the Law, and he is the Law:
In his hand are the deep places of the earth;
The strength of the hills is his also.
The sea is his, and he made it,
And his hands formed the dry land
Come, let us worship and bow down,
Let us kneel before the Heavenly Father,
For he is the Law,
And we are the people of his pasture,

And the sheep of his hand.
With songs of gladness the children of Light
Invoke the Holy Law:
Sickness flies away before it,
Death flies away,
Ignorance flies away.
Pride, scorn, and hot fever,
Slander, discord, and evil,
All anger and violence,
And lying words of falsehood,
All fly away before the power of the Holy Law.
Here is the Law
Which will smite all sickness,
Which will smite all death,
Which will smite the oppressors of men,
Which will smite pride,
Which will smite scorn,
Which will smite hot fevers,
Which will smite all slanders,
Which will smite all discords,
Which will smite the worst of evil,
Which will banish ignorance from the earth.
We bless the invocation and prayer,
The strength and vigor of the Holy Law.
We invoke the spirit, conscience, and soul
Of the Children of Light who teach the Law,
Who struggle in the kingdom of darkness
To bring the light of the Law to the Sons of Men.
We bless that victory
Of good thoughts, good words, and good deeds,
Which make strong the foundations of the Kingdom of Light.
Let the Sons of Men who think, speak, and do
All good thoughts, words, and deeds

Inhabit heaven as their home.
And let those who think, speak, and do
Evil thoughts, words, and deeds
Abide in chaos.
Purity is for man, next to life,
The greatest of good:
That purity is in the Holy Law,
Which maketh grass to grow upon the mountains,
And maketh clean the hearts of men.
With good thoughts, good words, and good deeds
Clean shall be the fire,
Clean the water,
Clean the earth,
Clean the stars, the moon, and the sun,
Clean the faithful man and the faithful woman,
Clean the boundless, eternal Light,
Clean the Kingdom of the Earthly Mother
And the Kingdom of the Heavenly Father,
Clean the good things made by the Law,
Whose offspring is the Holy Creation.
To obtain the treasures of the material world,
O sons of men,
Forego not the world of the Law.
For he who, to obtain the treasures
Of the material world,
Destroyeth in him the world of the Law,
Such an one shall possess neither force of life
Nor the Law,
Neither the Celestial Light.
But he who walks with the angels,
And who followeth the Holy Law,
He shall obtain everything good:
He shall enter the Eternal Sea

Where standeth the Tree of Life.
The Communions of the Law are perfect,
Converting the soul from darkness to light;
The testimony of the Law is sure,
Making wise the simple.
The statutes of the Law are right, rejoicing the heart;
The commandment of the Law is pure,
Enlightening the eyes.
The truth of the Law is clean, enduring forever.
Let the Children of Light triumph everywhere
Between the Heavens and the Earth!
Let us breathe the Holy Law in our prayer:
How beautiful are thy tabernacles,
O Heavenly Father!
My soul longeth, yea, even fainteth
For the Tree of Life
That standeth in the middle of the Eternal Sea.
My heart and my flesh crieth out for the living God.
Yea, the sparrow hath found a house,
And the swallow a nest for herself,
Where she may lay her young.
The Children of Light
Who labor in the Garden of the Brotherhood
Abide in the Holy Law:
Blessed are they who dwell therein!

THE ANGELS

The Heavenly Father
Gave his angels charge
Concerning thee:
And in their hands
They shall bear thee up,
Even unto the Tree of Life
That standeth in the midst
Of the Eternal Sea ...

For the wisdom of the Law,
For the unconquerable power of the Law,
And for the vigor of health,
For the Glory of the Heavenly Father
And the Earthly Mother,
And for all the boons and remedies
Of the Sevenfold Peace,
Do we worship the Holy Angels,
Our efforts for whom
And Communions to whom
Make us good in the eyes of Heavenly Father.
The Law is fulfilled according to the angels,
The Bright and Holy Ones,
Whose looks perform their wish,
Strong, lordly,
Who are undecaying and holy,
Who are seven and seven all of one Thought,
Who are seven and seven all of one Speech,
Who are seven and seven all of one Deed.
Whose Thought is the same,
Whose Speech is the same,

Whose Deed is the same,
Whose Father is the same,
Namely, the Heavenly Father!
The Angels who see one another's souls,
Who bring the Kingdom of the Earthly Mother
And the Kingdom of the Heavenly Father
To the Children of Light
Who labor in the Garden of the Brotherhood.
The Angels who are the Makers and Governors,
The Shapers and Overseers,
The Keepers and Preservers of the abundant Earth!
And of all Creations of the Heavenly Father.
We invoke the good, the strong, the beneficent
Angels of the Heavenly Father and the Earthly Mother!
That of the Light!
That of the Sky!
That of the Waters!
That of the Earth!
That of the Plants!
That of the Children of Light!
That of the Eternal Holy Creation!
We worship the angels
Who first listened unto the thought and teaching
Of the Heavenly Father,
Of whom the angels formed the seed of the nations.
We worship the angels
Who first touched the brow of our Father Enoch,
And guided the Children of Light
Through the seven and seven Paths
Which lead to the Tree of Life
That standeth forever in the midst of the Eternal Sea.
We worship all the angels,
The good, heroic, and bounteous angels,

*Of the bodily world of the Earthly Mother,
And those of the Invisible Realms,
Those in the Celestial Worlds of the Heavenly Father.
We worship the ever blessing immortal Angels,
The brilliant ones of splendorous countenance,
The lofty and devoted creatures of the Heavenly Father,
They who are imperishable and Holy.
We worship the resplendent, the glorious,
The bountiful Holy Angels,
Who rule aright, and who adjust all things rightly.
Hear the glad voices of the Children of Light,
Who sing the praise of the Holy Angels
As they labor in the Garden of the Brotherhood:
We sing with gladness to the waters, land, and plants,
To this earth and to the heavens,
To the holy wind, and the holy sun and moon,
To the eternal stars without beginning,
And to all the holy creatures of the Heavenly Father.
We sing with gladness unto the Holy Law,
Which is the Heavenly Order,
To the days and to the nights,
To the years and to the seasons
Which are the pillars of the Heavenly Order.
We worship the Angels of the Day,
And the Angels of the Month,
Those of the Years, and those of the Seasons,
All the good, the heroic,
The ever blessing immortal Angels
Who maintain and preserve the Heavenly Order.
We desire to approach the mighty Angels,
All the Angels of the Heavenly Order,
Because of the Holy Law,
Which is the best of all good.*

We do present these thoughts well thought,
These words well spoken,
These deeds well done,
To the bountiful, immortal Angels,
Those who exercise their right rule.
We do present these offerings
To the Angels of the Day,
And the Angels of the Night,
The ever-living, the ever-helpful,
Who dwell eternally with the Divine Mind.
May the good and heroic and bountiful
Angels of the Heavenly Father
And the Earthly Mother
Walk with their holy feet
In the Garden of the Brotherhood,
And may they go hand in hand with us
With the healing virtues of their blessed gifts,
As widespread as the earth,
As far-spread as the rivers,
As high-reaching as the sun,
For the furtherance of the betterment of man,
And for abundant growth.
It is they, the Holy Angels,
Who shall restore the World!
Which will thenceforth never grow old and never die!
Never decaying, ever living, and ever increasing.
Then Life and Immortality will come
And the World will be restored!
Creation will grow deathless,
The Kingdom of the Heavenly Father will prosper,
And evil shall have perished!

THE BROTHERHOOD

Behold, how good and how pleasant it is
For the Children of Light
To dwell together in unity!
For the Brotherhood
The Heavenly Father
Hath commanded the Law.
Even life forevermore.

The Law was planted in the Garden of the Brotherhood
To illumine the hearts of the Children of Light,
To make straight before them
The seven and seven paths leading to the Tree of Life
Which standeth in the midst of the Eternal Sea;
The Law was planted in the Garden of the Brotherhood,
That they might recognize
The spirits of truth and falsehood,
Truth born out of the spring of Light,
Falsehood from the well of darkness.
The dominion of all the Children of Truth
Is in the hands of the mighty Angels of Light,
So that they walk in the ways of Light.
The Children of Light are the servants of the Law,
And the Heavenly Father shall not forget them.
He hath blotted out their sins as a thick cloud;
He hath lit the candle of Truth within their hearts.
Sing, O ye heavens,
Shout, ye lower parts of the earth,
Break forth into singing, ye mountains,
O forest, and every tree therein:
For the Heavenly Father hath kindled his flame
In the hearts of the Children of Light,

And glorified himself in them.
The Holy Law of the Creator
Purifieth the followers of the Light
From every evil thought, word, and deed,
As a swift-rushing mighty wind
Doth cleanse the plain.
Let the child of Light who so desireth
Be taught the Holy Word,
During the first watch of the day and the last,
During the first watch of the night and the last,
That his mind may be increased in intelligence
And his soul wax strong in the Holy Law.
At the hour of dawn
He shall gaze upon the rising sun
And greet with joy his Earthly Mother.
At the hour of dawn
He shall wash his body in the cool water
And greet with joy his Earthly Mother.
At the hour of dawn
He shall breathe the fragrant air
And greet with joy his Earthly Mother.
And through the day
He shall labor with his brethren
In the Garden of the Brotherhood.
In the hour of twilight
He shall gather with his brothers,
And together they shall study the holy words
Of our fathers, and their fathers' fathers,
Even unto the words of our Father Enoch.
And when the stars are high in the heavens
He shall commune
With the holy Angels of the Heavenly Father.
And his voice shall be raised with gladness

Unto the most High, saying,
We worship the Creator,
The maker of all good things:
The Good Mind,
And of the Law,
Immortality,
And the Holy Fire of Life.
We do offer to the Law
The Wisdom of the Tongue,
Holy Speech, Deeds, and rightly-spoken Words.
Grant us, Heavenly Father,
That we may bring down abundance
To the world thou hast created,
That we may take away both hunger and thirst
From the world thou hast created,
That we may take away both old age and death
From the world thou hast created.
O good, most beneficent Heavenly Father!
Grant us that we may think
According to the Law,
That we may speak
According to the Law,
That we may do
According to the Law.
O Heavenly Father,
What is the invocation most worthy
In greatness and goodness?
It is that one, O Children of Light,
That one delivers
When waking up and rising from sleep,
At the same time professing
Good thoughts, good words, and good deeds,
And rejecting evil thoughts, evil words, and evil deeds.

The first step
That the soul of the Child of Light did make,
Placed him in the Good Thought Paradise,
The Holy Realm of Wisdom.
The second step
That the soul of the Child of Light did make,
Placed him in the Good Word Paradise,
The Holy Realm of Love.
The third step
That the soul of the Child of Light did make,
Placed him in the Good Deed Paradise,
The Holy Realm of Power.
The fourth step
That the soul of the Child of Light did make,
Placed him in the Endless Light.
The Heavenly Father knoweth the hearts
Of the Children of Light,
And their inheritance shall be forever.
They shall not be afraid in the evil time:
And in the days of famine they shall be satisfied.
For with them is the Fountain of Life,
And the Heavenly Father forsaketh not his children.
Their souls shall breathe forever and ever,
And their forms shall be endowed with Eternal Life.
Blessings on the Children of Light
Who have cast their lot with the Law,
That walk truthfully in all their ways.
May the Law bless them with all good
And keep them from all evil,
And illumine their hearts
With insight into the things of life
And grace them with knowledge of things eternal.

TREES

Go towards the high-growing Trees,
And before one of them
Which is beautiful, high-growing, and mighty,
Say thou these words:
Hail be unto Thee!
O good living Tree,
Made by the Creator.

In the days of old, when the Creation was young,
The earth was filled with giant trees,
Whose branches soared above the clouds,
And in them dwelled our Ancient Fathers,
They who walked with the angels,
And who lived by the Holy Law.
In the shadow of their branches all men lived in peace,
And wisdom and knowledge was theirs,
And the revelation of the Endless Light.
Through their forests flowed the Eternal River,
And in the center stood the Tree of Life,
And it was not hidden from them.
They ate from the table of the Earthly Mother,
And slept in the arms of the Heavenly Father,
And their covenant was for eternity with the Holy Law.
In that time the trees were the brothers of men,
And their span on the earth was very long,
As long as the Eternal River,
Which flowed without ceasing
From the Unknown Spring.
Now the desert sweeps the earth with burning sand,
The giant trees are dust and ashes,

And the wide river is a pool of mud.
For the sacred covenant with the Creator
Was broken by the Sons of Men,
And they were banished from their home of trees.
Now the path leading to the Tree of Life
Is hidden from the eyes of men,
And sorrow fills the empty sky
Where once the lofty branches soared.
Now into the burning desert
Come the Children of Light,
To labor in the Garden of the Brotherhood.
The seed they plant in the barren soil
Will become a mighty forest,
And trees shall multiply
And spread their wings of green
Until the whole earth be covered once again.
The whole earth shall be a garden,
And the tall trees shall cover the land
In that day shall sing the Children of Light a new song:
My brother, Tree!
Let me not hide myself from thee,
But let us share the breath of life
Which our Earthly Mother hath given to us.
More beautiful than the finest jewel
Of the rugmaker's art,
Is the carpet of green leaves under my bare feet;
More majestic than the silken canopy of the rich merchant,
Is the tent of branches above my head,
Through which the bright stars give light.
The wind among the leaves of the cypress
Maketh a sound like unto a chorus of angels.
Through the rugged oak and royal cedar
The Earthly Mother hath sent a message of Eternal Life

To the Heavenly Father.
My prayer goeth forth unto the tall trees:
And their branches reaching skyward
Shall carry my voice to the Heavenly Father.
For each child, thou shalt plant a tree,
That the womb of thy Earthly Mother
Shall bring forth life,
As the womb of woman doth bring forth life.
He who doth destroy a tree
Hath cut off his own limbs.
Thus shall sing the Children of Light,
When the earth again shall be a garden:
Holy Tree, divine gift of the Law!
Thy majesty reunites all those
Who have strayed from their true home,
Which is the Garden of the Brotherhood.
All men will become brothers once again
Under thy spreading branches.
As the Heavenly Father hath loved all his children,
So shall we love and care for the trees
That grow in our land,
So shall we keep and protect them,
That they may grow tall and strong,
And fill the earth again with their beauty.
For the trees are our brothers,
And as brothers,
We shall guard and love one another.

STARS

The white, shining,
Far-seen Stars!
The piercing, health-bringing,
Far-piercing Stars!
Their shining rays,
Their brightness and glory
Are all, through thy Holy Law,
The Speakers of thy praise,
O Heavenly Father!

Over the face of heaven
Did the Heavenly Father hurl his might:
And lo! He did leave a River of Stars in his wake!
We invoke the bright and glorious Stars
That wash away all things of fear
And bring health and life unto all Creations.
We invoke the bright and glorious Stars
To which the Heavenly Father
Hath given a thousand senses,
The glorious Stars that have within themselves
The Seed of Life and of Water.
Unto the bright and glorious Stars
Do we offer up an Invocation:
With wisdom, power, and love,
With speech, deeds, and rightly-spoken words,
Do we sacrifice unto the bright and glorious Stars
That fly towards the Heavenly Sea
As swiftly as the arrow
Darteth through heavenly Space.
We invoke the bright and glorious Stars,
That stand out beautiful,

*Spreading comfort and joy
As they commune within themselves.
The Holy Works,
The Stars, the Suns, and the many-colored Dawn
Which bringeth on the Light of Days,
Are all, through their Heavenly Order,
The Speakers of thy praise,
O thou great giver, the Holy Law!
We invoke the Lord of the Stars,
The Angel of Light,
The ever-awake!
Who taketh possession
of the beautiful, wide-expanding Law,
Greatly and powerfully,
And whose face looketh over
All the seven and seven Kingdoms of the Earth;
Who is swift amongst the swift,
Bountiful amongst the bounteous,
Strong amongst the strong,
The Giver of Increase,
The Giver of Sovereignty,
The Giver of Cheerfulness and Bliss.
We invoke the Lord of the Stars,
The Angel of Light,
Who is truth-speaking,
With a thousand ears and ten thousand eyes,
With full knowledge, strong, and ever-awake.
The Heavenly Order pervades all things pure,
Whose are the Stars,
In whose Light the glorious Angels are clothed.
Great is our Heavenly Father, and of great power:
His understanding is infinite.
He telleth the number of the stars;*

He calleth them all by their names.
Behold the height of the stars!
How high they are!
Yet the Heavenly Father doth hold them in his palms,
As we do sift the sand in ours.
He who knoweth not the Holy Law
Is as a wandering star
In the darkness of an unknown sky.
Thinkest thou there is but one way
To see the firmament?
Suppose ye the stars were but broken places in the sky
Through which the glory of heaven is revealed
In fragments of blazing light!
In the purple night
Traversed by the continual Stars
Shall the souls of the Children of Light
Take wing and join the Angels of the Heavenly Father.
Then shall the Eternal Sea
Reflect the shining glory of the heavens,
And the branches of the Tree of Life reach to the Stars.
Then shall the Kingdom of Heaven
Fill all the earth with Glory,
And the shining Stars of the most High
Shall blaze within the hearts of the Children of Light
And warm and comfort the seeking Sons of Men.

THE MOON

Unto the luminous Moon
Which keepeth within itself
The seed of many species,
Let there be invocation
With sacrifice and prayer ...

When the Light of the Moon waxeth warmer,
Golden-hued plants grow up from the earth
During the season of Spring.
We sacrifice unto the New Moons
And unto the Full Moons;
The crescent of the New Moon is full of holy Peace
We sacrifice unto the Angel of Peace.
The radiant and luminous Moon
Keepeth within itself the seed:
The bright, the glorious,
The water-giving,
The warmth-giving,
The wisdom-giving,
The thoughtfulness-giving,
The freshness-giving,
The healing one, the Moon of Peace!
With silent and peace-giving light
The Moon doth shine
Upon the pastures, the abodes,
The waters, the lands, and the plants
Of our earthly garden.
The Moon and the Sun,
The holy Wind and the Stars without beginning,
Self-determined and self-moved,
All are regulators of the Holy Order,

*of the days and nights, of the months and years.
The face of the Moon doth change its aspect,
Yet is ever the same:
As the Holy Law doth reveal a different face
To each of the Children of Light,
Yet is unchanged in its Essence.
We invoke the New Moon and the Moon that is waning,
And the Full Moon that scattereth the Night,
And the yearly festivals and the seasons of the Heavenly Father.
For it was he who gavest the moon
Her increase and her decrease,
That through her we might know the movements
Of the day and of the night.
Thou silver and luminous moon!
We are grateful that we may look on thee,
And see in thy reflection
The blessed face of our Earthly Mother.
Among the world of the Sons of Men,
The Brothers of Light are flames of radiance,
As the stars pale in the presence of the bright and shining moon.
The moon walketh in brightness across the sky,
And delight in the Holy Law doth fill our hearts.
Peace, Peace, Peace,
Holy Angel of Peace,
Illumine the silver moon with thy holiness,
That all may look upon its beauty
And feel thy eternal Peace.
The desert sky is blue with night,
And we see the first ray of the New Moon
Chaste and beautiful.
Then do the Brothers greet one another,
Saying, "Peace be with thee!
Peace be with thee!"*

PSALMS OF PRAISE AND THANKSGIVING

I am grateful, Heavenly Father,
For thou hast raised me to an eternal height,
And I walk in the wonders of the plain.
Thou gavest me guidance
To reach thine eternal company
From the depths of the earth.
Thou hast purified my body
To join the army of the Angels of the earth
And my spirit to reach
The congregation of the Heavenly Angels.
Thou gavest man eternity
To praise at dawn and dusk
Thy works and wonders
in joyful song.

O all ye works of the Heavenly Order,
Bless ye the Law:
Praise and exalt the Law above all forever.
O ye heavens, bless ye the Law:
Praise and exalt the Law above all forever.
O ye Angels of the Heavenly Father,
And ye Angels of the Earthly Mother,
Bless ye the Law:
Praise and exalt the Law above all forever.
O all ye waters that be above the heavens,
Bless ye the Law.
O all ye powers of the Holy Angels, bless ye the Law.
O ye sun and moon, bless ye the Law.
O ye stars of heaven, bless ye the Law.
O every shower and dew, bless ye the Law.
O all ye winds, bless ye the Law.

O ye fire and heat, bless ye the Law.
O ye winter and summer, bless ye the Law.
O ye light and darkness, bless ye the Law.
O ye dews and storms of snow, bless ye the Law.
O ye nights and days, bless ye the Law.
O ye lightnings and clouds, bless ye the Law.
O ye mountains and little hills, bless ye the Law.
O all ye things that grow on the earth, bless ye the Law.
O ye fountains, bless ye the Law.
O ye seas and rivers, bless ye the Law.
O ye whales, and all that move in the waters,
Bless ye the Law.
O all ye fowls of the air, bless ye the Law.
O all ye beasts and cattle, bless ye the Law.
O ye children of men, bless ye the Law.
O ye spirits and souls of the Children of Light,
Bless ye the Law.
O ye holy and humble workers
In the Garden of the Brotherhood, bless ye the Law.
O let the whole earth bless the Law!
O give thanks unto the Heavenly Father,
And bless ye his Law.
O all ye that worship the Law,
Give praise unto the Heavenly Father
And the Earthly Mother,
And all the Holy Angels,
And give unto them thanks,
For the Law endureth forever.
We worship the Law by day and by night.
Hail to the Heavenly Father!
Hail to the Earthly Mother!
Hail to the Holy Angels!
Hail to the Children of Light!

Hail to our holy Father Enoch!
Hail to the whole of Holy Creation
That was, that is, or ever shall be!
We sacrifice unto the bright and glorious stars,
We sacrifice unto the sovereign sky,
We sacrifice unto boundless time,
We sacrifice unto the good Law
Of the worshipers of the Creator,
Of the Children of Light
Who labor in the Garden of the Brotherhood;
We sacrifice unto the way of the Holy Law.
We sacrifice unto all the Holy Angels
Of the world unseen;
We sacrifice unto all the Holy Angels
Of the material world.
O give thanks unto the Heavenly Father, for he is good,
O give thanks unto the God of the Angels,
O give thanks unto the Lord of Light,
For his mercy endureth forever.
To him who alone doeth great wonders,
To him that by wisdom made the heavens,
To him that stretched out the earth above the waters,
To him that made great lights in the heavens,
To him that made the sun to rule by day,
And the moon and stars to rule by night,
Give unending praise and thanksgiving,
For his mercy endureth forever.
And we do worship the ancient and holy religion,
Which was instituted at the Creation,
Which was on the earth in the time of the Great Trees;
The holy religion of the Creator,
The resplendent and the glorious,
Revealed unto our Father Enoch.

We do worship the Creator,
And the Fire of Life,
And the good Waters which are Holy,
And the resplendent Sun and the Moon,
And the lustrous, glorious Stars;
And most of all we do worship the Holy Law,
Which the Creator, our Heavenly Father,
Hath given to us.
It is the Law which maketh holy our dwelling place,
Which is the wide green earth.
Praise ye the Law!
The Law healeth the broken in heart,
And bindeth up their wounds.
Great is the Law, and of great power;
The understanding of the Law is infinite.
The Law lifteth up the meek,
And casteth the wicked down to the ground.
Sing unto the Law with thanksgiving,
Sing praise upon the harp unto the Law,
Which covereth the heaven with clouds,
Which prepareth rain for the earth,
Which maketh grass to grow upon the mountains.
We praise aloud the well-thought Thought,
The Word well-spoken,
And the Deed well-done.
We will come to thee, O ye bountiful immortals!
We will come to thee, extolling and invoking thee,
Angels of the Heavenly Father and the Earthly Mother!
We do worship the Holy Lord of the Heavenly Order,
The Creator of all good creatures of the earth.
And we do worship the utterances of our Father Enoch,
And his ancient, pure religion,
His faith and his lore, older than the beginning of time.

We will sing unto the Law as long as we live,
We will sing praise unto our Heavenly Father
While we have our being,
While the Garden of the Brotherhood doth endure.
Our Communions with the angels shall be sweet;
We will be glad in the Law.
Bless thou the Law, O my soul.
Praise ye the Holy Law.
The Children of Light love the Law,
Because the Law heareth our voices
And our supplications.
An all-hearing ear hath the Law inclined unto us,
Therefore will we call upon the Law as long as we live.
The Law hath delivered our souls from death,
Our eyes from tears, and our feet from falling.
We will walk before the Law in the land of the living:
In the paths of the Infinite Garden of the Brotherhood.
The days of the Sons of Men are as grass;
As flowers of the field, so they flourish.
For the wind passeth over them, and they are gone:
But the mercy of the Law is from everlasting
To everlasting upon them that follow it.
Bless the Heavenly Father, all ye his angels;
Ye ministers of his, that do his pleasure.
Bless the Lord, all his works,
In all places of his dominion:
Bless the Lord, O my soul.
O Heavenly Father, thou art very great!
Thou art clothed with honor and majesty.
Who coverest thyself with light as with a garment,
Who stretchest out the heavens like a curtain,
Who layeth the beams of his chambers in the waters,
Who maketh the clouds his chariot,

Who walketh upon the wings of the wind,
Who maketh his angels' spirits,
His Children of Light a flaming fire
To kindle the Truth in the hearts of the Sons of en,
Who laid the foundations of the earth.
Bless the Heavenly Father, O my soul!

LAMENTS

Out of the depths have I cried unto thee, O Lord.
Lord, hear my voice!

Hear my prayer, O Lord,
And let my cry come unto thee.
Hide not thy face from me
In the day when I am in trouble;
Incline thine ear unto me;
In the day when I call, answer me speedily.
For my days are consumed like smoke,
And my bones are burned as a hearth.
My heart is smitten, and withered like grass;
So that I forget to eat my bread.
By reason of the voice of my groaning,
My bones cleave to my skin.
I am like a pelican of the wilderness;
I am like an owl of the desert.
I watch, and am as a sparrow,
Alone upon the housetop.
My days are like a shadow that declineth;
And I am withered like grass.
O my God, take me not away in the midst of my days:
The heavens are the work of thy hands.
They shall perish, but thou shalt endure.
The first step taken
By the soul of the wicked man,
Laid him in the evil thought hell.
The second step take
By the soul of the wicked man,
Laid him in the evil word hell.
The third step taken

By the soul of the wicked man,
Laid him in the evil deed hell.
The fourth step taken
By the soul of the wicked man,
Laid him in endless darkness.
I know that thou canst do all things,
And that no purpose of thine can be restrained.
Now mine eye seeth thee,
Wherefore I abhor myself,
And repent in dust and ashes.
For the wicked Sons of Men
Have sinned against themselves,
And their hell of evil thoughts, evil words, and evil deeds
Is a hell of their own making.
But my anguish and my bitter tears
Are for our ancient fathers,
Who sinned against the Creator,
And were banished
From the Holy Kingdom of the Great Trees.
Wherefore I weep, and hide my face in sorrow,
For the beauty of the Lost Garden,
And the vanished sweetness of the song of the Bird,
Who sang in the branches of the Tree of Life.
Have mercy upon me, O God,
And cleanse me from my sin.
The joy of our hearts is ceased,
Our dance is turned into mourning.
The crown is fallen from our head:
Woe unto us, that we have sinned!
For this, our heart is faint,
For these things, our eyes are dim.
Thou, O Heavenly Father, remainest forever,
Thy throne from generation to generation.

Wherefore dost thou forget us forever,
And forsake us so long time?
Turn thou us unto thee, O Lord,
Renew our days as of old.
Where there is no righteousness or compassion,
There wild beasts of the desert shall lie;
And their houses shall be full of doleful creatures.
And owls shall dwell there,
And satyrs shall dance there.
And the wild beasts shall cry in their desolate houses.
Wash me, O Lord, and I shall be whiter than snow.
Make me to hear joy and gladness;
Hide thy face from my sins,
And blot out all mine iniquities.
Create in me a clean heart, O God;
And renew a right spirit within me.
Cast me not away from thy presence;
And take not thy holy spirit from me.
Restore unto me the joy of thy Infinite Garden,
And uphold me with thy Holy Angels.
Let me drive away all evil things
And all uncleanness,
From the fire, the water,
The earth, the trees,
From the faithful man and the faithful woman,
From the stars, the moon, the sun,
From the boundless Light,
And from all good things,
Made by thee, O Heavenly Father,
Whose offspring is the Holy Law.
By the rivers of Babylon,
There we sat down, yea, we wept,
When we remembered Zion.

We hanged our harps upon the willows.
How shall we sing the Lord's song
In a wicked land?
If I forget thee, O Jerusalem,
Let my right hand forget her cunning.
If I do not remember thee,
Let my tongue cleave to the roof of my mouth;
For Babylon is the slavery in the world,
And Zion is the freedom in the Brotherhood.
O Lord, to thee will I cry!
For the fire hath devoured the pastures of the wilderness,
And the flame hath burned all the trees of the field.
The beasts of the field cry also unto thee:
For the rivers of waters are dried up,
And the fire hath devoured
The pastures of the wilderness.
Let all the inhabitants of the land tremble:
For the day of the Lord cometh,
For it is nigh at hand;
A day of darkness and gloominess,
A day of clouds and of thick darkness,
A day when the earth shall quake,
And the heavens shall tremble.
The sun and the moon shall be dark,
And the stars shall withdraw their shining.
Out of the depths will we cry unto thee, O Lord!
Lord, hear thou our voices!

PROPHECIES

Hearken unto me, my people,
And give ear unto me!
Lift up thine eyes to the heavens,
And look upon the earth beneath:
For the heavens shall vanish away like smoke,
And the earth shall wax old like a garment,
And they that dwell therein
Shall die in like manner:
But my Kingdom shall be forever,
And my Law shall not be abolished.

And in that day hell shall enlarge herself,
And open her mouth without measure:
And the glory, the pride, and the pomp of the wicked
Shall descend into it.
And the mean man shall be brought down,
And the mighty man shall be humbled
As the fire devoureth the stubble,
And the flame consumeth the chaff;
So their root shall be as rottenness,
And their blossom shall go up as dust.
Because they have cast away
The Holy Law of the Heavenly Order,
And despised the word of the Children of Light.
And in that day, one will look unto the land
And behold only darkness and sorrow,
And the light in the heavens shall be darkened.
The leaders of the people shall cause them to err,
And they that are led of them shall be destroyed.
For everyone is an hypocrite and an evildoer,
And every mouth speaketh folly.

Wickedness burneth as the fire:
It shall devour the briars and thorns.
It shall kindle in the thickets of the forest,
And shall mount up like the lifting up of smoke.
Through the wrath of the Law
Shall the land be darkened,
For this hath man wrought upon himself.
And the people shall be as the fuel of the fire:
No man shall spare his brother.
Woe unto them that have kept not the Holy Law!
Woe unto the crown of pride!
Woe unto those who lust after the things of the world,
And corrupt themselves with wrongdoing,
Who err in vision, and stumble in judgment:
For they are a rebellious people, a lying people,
People who will not hear the Law of the Lord:
Which say to the seers, see not,
And to the Prophets, prophesy not unto us right things,
But speak unto us smooth things, prophesy deceits.
Woe unto them that decree unrighteous decrees,
And that write grievousness which they have prescribed.
Woe unto them that join house to house,
That lay field to field,
Till there be no place that a man may be alone
In the midst of the earth!
Woe unto them that rise up early in the morning,
Not to commune with the angels,
But to follow strong drink, and continue until night,
Till the fumes of the wine inflame them!
Woe unto them that call evil good, and good evil,
That put darkness for light, and light for darkness.
Woe unto them
That turn aside the needy from judgment,

And take away the right from the poor,
That make of widows their prey, and rob the fatherless!
Wherefore it shall come to pass
That the hand of the Lord shall lop the bough
With the judgment of the Law,
And the high ones of stature shall be hewn down
And the haughty shall be humbled.
Howl ye, for the day of the Law is at hand;
It shall come as a destruction from the Almighty.
Therefore shall all hands be faint,
And every man's heart shall melt.
And they shall be afraid:
Pangs and sorrows shall take hold of them;
They shall be in pain as a woman that travaileth:
They shall be amazed one at another:
Their faces shall be as flames.
Behold, the day of the Lord cometh
Cruel, both with wrath and fierce anger,
To lay the land desolate:
And he shall destroy the sinners thereof out of it.
It shall come to pass in that day,
That the Lord shall punish the host of the high ones,
And the kings of the earth upon the earth.
And they shall be gathered together,
As prisoners are gathered in the pit,
And shall be shut up in the prison.
And the Lord shall come forth out of his place,
And will come down,
And tread upon the high places of the earth.
And the mountains shall be molten under him,
And the valleys shall be cleft, as wax before the fire,
As the waters pour down a steep place.
Then the moon shall vanish, and the sun be obscured.

And the stars of heaven and the constellations thereof
Shall not give their light:
The sun shall be darkened in its going forth,
And the moon shall not cause her light to shine.
And the Lord will shake the heavens,
And the earth shall remove out of her place,
In the day of the wrath of the Law,
In the day of the fierce anger of the Lord.
And the shining cities shall be laid waste,
And wild beasts of the desert shall lie there;
The hay shall wither away, the grass shall fail,
And in all the earth there shall be no green thing.
In that day shall the strong cities
Be as a forsaken bough,
And a tempest of hail
Shall sweep away the refuge of lies,
And the angry waters
Shall overflow the hiding place of the wicked.
And there shall be upon every high mountain,
And upon every high hill,
Rivers and streams of waters
In the day of the great slaughter,
When the towers fall.
In that day shall the light of the moon
Be as the light of the sun,
And the light of the sun shall be sevenfold.
Behold, the name of the Law cometh from far,
Burning with hot anger,
And the burden thereof is heavy:
The lips of the Lord are full of indignation,
And his tongue is as a devouring fire.
He shall show the strength of his arm,
With the flame of consuming fire,

With scattering, and tempest, and hailstones.
The land shall be utterly emptied, and utterly spoiled,
For the Sons of Men have turned away from the Law.
The city of confusion is broken down:
Every house is shut up, that no man may come in.
There is a crying and wailing in the streets:
All joy is darkened, the mirth of the land is gone.
And it shall come to pass,
That he who fleeth from the noise of the fear
Shall fall into the pit;
And he that cometh up out of the midst of the pit
Shall be taken in the snare:
For the windows from on high are open,
And the foundations of the earth do shake.
The earth is utterly broken down,
The earth is clean dissolved,
The earth is moved exceedingly.
Then the moon shall be confounded,
The sun shall be ashamed,
And the earth shall reel to and fro like a drunkard,
And shall fall, and shall not rise again.
And all the host of heaven shall be dissolved,
And the heavens shall be rolled together as a scroll:
And all their host shall fall down,
As the leaf falleth off from the vine,
And as a falling fig from the fig tree.
The waters shall fail from the sea,
And the rivers shall be wasted and dried up.
Streams of water shall be turned into pitch,
And the dust thereof into brimstone,
And the land thereof shall become burning pitch.
And the smoke shall not be quenched by night or day,
And no man shall pass through it.

*But the cormorant and the bittern
Shall possess the land;
The owl also, and the raven shall dwell in it.
And there shall stretch out upon it
The line of confusion, and the stones of emptiness.
They shall call the nobles thereof to the kingdom,
But none shall be there,
And all her princes shall be nothing.
And thorns shall come up in her palaces,
Nettles and brambles in the fortresses thereof:
And it shall be an habitation of dragons,
And a court for owls.
The ambassadors of peace shall weep bitterly,
And the highways shall lie waste.
The glory of the forests shall be consumed,
And the fruitful field;
Yea, the trees shall be so few,
That a child may count them.
Behold, the day shall come,
That all that is in the earth,
And all that which thy fathers have laid up in store,
Shall be carried up in smoke,
For ye have forgotten thy Heavenly Father
And thy Earthly Mother,
And ye have broken the Holy Law.
Oh that thou wouldst rend the heavens,
That thou wouldst come down,
That the mountains might flow down at thy presence.
When thy hand showed forth the power of thy Law
Thou camest down in fury:
The mountains flowed down at thy presence,
And the melting fires burned.
Behold, thou art wroth, for we have sinned.*

We are like the troubled sea, when it cannot rest,
Whose waters cast up mire and dirt.
We trust in vanity, and speak lies;
Our feet run to evil,
Wasting and destruction are in our paths.
We grope for the wall like the blind,
We stumble at noonday as in the night,
We are in desolate places as dead men.
But now, O Heavenly Father, thou art our father:
We are the clay, and thou our potter,
And we are all thy people.
Thy holy cities are a wilderness,
Thy forests are consumed,
All thy earth is a desolation.
Our holy and beautiful house,
Where our fathers praised thee,
Is burned up with fire.
Even the ancient lore of our Father Enoch
Is trampled in the dust and ashes.
And I beheld the earth, and, lo,
It was without form, and void;
And the heavens, and they had no light.
I beheld the mountains, and, lo, they trembled,
And all the hills moved lightly.
I beheld, and, lo, there was no man,
And all the birds of the heavens
I beheld, and, lo, the fruitful place was a wilderness,
And all the cities thereof were broken down
At the presence of the Lord, and by his fierce anger.
For thus hath the Lord said,
The whole land shall be desolate;
Yet will I not make a full end.
Behold, the hand of the Law is not shortened,

That it cannot save;
Neither is the ear of the Law heavy,
That it cannot hear:
From out of the desert shall I bring forth a seed,
And the seed shall be planted
In the Garden of the Brotherhood,
And it shall flourish,
And the Children of Light shall cover the barren land
With tall grass and trees bearing fruit.
And they shall build the old waste places:
They shall repair the waste cities
The desolations of many generations.
They shall be called the repairers of the breach,
And the restorers of paths to dwell in.
They shall be a crown of glory on the head of the Lord
And a royal diadem in the hand of the Law.
The wilderness and the solitary place
Shall be glad for them,
And the desert shall rejoice, and blossom as the rose.
It shall blossom abundantly,
And rejoice even with joy and singing.
The eyes of the blind shall be opened,
And the ears of the deaf shall be unstopped
Then shall the lame man leap as an hart
And the tongue of the dumb shall sing
For in the wilderness shall waters break out,
And flowing streams in the desert.
And the parched ground shall become a pool,
And the thirsty land, springs of water.
And a highway shall be there, and a way,
And it shall be called the Way of the Law:
The unclean shall not pass over it,
But it shall be for the Children of Light

*To cross over the Eternal River unto the hidden place
Where standeth the Tree of Life.
And the children of men shall return to the earth,
And come unto the Infinite Garden
With songs and everlasting joy upon their heads:
They shall obtain joy and gladness,
And sorrow and sighing shall flee away,
And it shall come to pass in the last days,
That the mountain of the Lord's house
Shall be established in the top of the mountains,
And shall be exalted above the hills;
And all the Sons of Men of the earth shall flow unto it.
And many people shall go and say,
"Come ye, and let us go up to the mountain of the Lord,
To the tabernacle of the Holy Law,
And the Holy Angels will teach us
of the ways of the Heavenly Father
And the Earthly Mother,
And we will walk in the paths of the righteous:
For out of the Garden of the Brotherhood
Shall go forth the Law,
And the word of the Lord from the Children of Light.
And the Lord shall judge among the nations,
And shall rebuke many people:
And they shall beat their swords into plowshares,
And their spears into pruninghooks:
Nation shall not lift up sword against nation,
Neither shall they learn war any more.
Hear the voices of the Brothers,
Which cry aloud in the wilderness:
Prepare ye the way of the Law!
Make straight in the desert a highway for our God!
Every valley shall be exalted,*

And every mountain and hill shall be made low:
And the crooked shall be made straight,
And the rough places plain:
And the voice of the Heavenly Father shall be heard:
1, even I, am the Law; and beside me there is no other.
Yea, before the day was I am he:
And there is none that can deliver out of my hand.
Hearken unto me, O Children of Light!
I am he; I am the first, I also am the last.
Mine hand also hath laid the foundation of the earth,
And my right hand hath spanned the heavens.
Hearken unto me, O Children of Light!
Ye that know righteousness,
My children in whose hearts is my Law:
Ye shall go out with joy, and be led forth with peace:
The mountains and the hills
Shall break forth before you into singing,
And all the trees of the field shall clap their hands.
Arise, shine, O Children of Light!
For my Light is come upon thee,
And thou shalt make the Glory of the Law
To rise upon the new earth!"

THE ESSENE GOSPEL OF PEACE
Book Four
The Teachings of the Elect

CONTENTS

Preface..257

The Essene Communions......................................259

The Gift of Life in the Humble Grass........................269

The Sevenfold Peace..279

The Holy Streams..291

PREFACE

It was in 1928 that Edmond Bordeaux Szekely first published his translation of Book One of *The Essene Gospel of Peace,* an ancient manuscript he had found in the Secret Archives of the Vatican as the result of limitless patience, faultless scholarship, and unerring intuition, a story told in his book, *The Discovery of the Essene Gospel of Peace.* The English version of this ancient manuscript appeared in 1937, and ever since, the little volume has traveled all over the world, appearing in different languages, and gaining every year more and more readers, until now, still with no commercial advertisement, over a million copies have been sold in the United States alone. It was not until almost fifty years after the first French translation that Book Two and Book Three appeared, and these also have now become classics of the Essene literature.

Book Four, *The Teachings of the Elect,* will come as a surprise to those readers who are aware of Dr. Szekely's death in 1979. If I were also a philologist, or scholar, or archeologist, I might be able to provide some explanation. But I am only his faithful *famulus amanuensis,* and the instructions he left me were clear and explicit: "Two years after my death, you shall publish Book Four of *The Essene Gospel of Peace."* That was all, and I am now carrying out his wish.

This Book Four, *The Teachings of the Elect,* represents yet another fragment of the complete manuscript which exists in Aramaic in the Secret Archives of the Vatican and in old Slavonic in the Royal Library of the Habsburgs (now the property of the Austrian government). As to the reason for the delay in its publication, I can only surmise that Dr. Szekely wanted the vivid reality of these ageless truths to stand alone, unobscured even by the presence of the translator. He did say in his Preface to the first London edition of Book One in 1937 that "we have issued this part before the rest, because it is the part of which suffering humanity has most need today." Perhaps, in the same way, the troubled world of forty-four years later needs this fourth volume of *The Essene Gospel of Peace*.

Again the words of Dr. Szekely: "We have nothing to add to this text. It speaks for itself. The reader who studies the pages that follow with concentration, will feel the eternal vitality and powerful evidence of these profound truths which mankind needs today more urgently than ever before."

"And the truth shall bear witness of itself."

NORMA NILSSON BORDEAUX

Orosi, Costa Rica, 1981.

THE ESSENE COMMUNIONS

And it came to pass that Jesus gathered the Sons of Light by the shore of the river, to reveal to them that which had been hidden; for the space of seven years had passed, and each one was ripe for truth, as the flower opens from the bud when the Angels of Sun and Water bring it to its time of blossoming.

And all of them were unlike one to the other, for some were of age, and some had still the dew of youth on their cheeks, and some had been raised according to the traditions of their fathers, and others knew not who their father and mother had been. But all shared in a clearness of eye and a suppleness of body, for these were signs that for seven years they had walked with the Angels of the Earthly Mother and obeyed her laws. And for seven years the unknown Angels of the Heavenly Father had taught them through their sleeping hours. And now was the day come when they would enter the Brotherhood of the Elect and learn the hidden teachings of the Elders, even those of Enoch and before.

And Jesus led the Sons of Light to an ancient tree by the side of the river, and there he knelt at the place where the roots, gnarled and hoary with age, spread over the river edge. And the Sons of Light knelt also, and they did touch with reverence the trunk of the ancient tree, for it was taught to them that the trees are the Brothers of the Sons of Men. For their mother is the same, the Earthly Mother, whose blood runs in the sap of the tree and in the body of the Son of Man. And their father is the same, the Heavenly Father, whose laws are written in the branches of the tree, and whose laws are engraved in the forehead of the Son of Man.

And Jesus reached out his hands to the tree, and said: "Behold, the Tree of Life, which stands in the middle of the Eternal Sea. Look not only with the eyes of the body, but see with the eyes of the spirit the Tree of Life at a source of running streams; at a living spring in a land of drought. See the eternal garden of wonders, and at its center the Tree of Life, Mystery of Mysteries, growing everlasting branches for eternal planting, to sink their roots into the stream of life from an eternal source. See with the eyes of the spirit the Angels of Day and the Angels of Night which protect the fruits with flames of Eternal Light burning every way.

"See, oh Sons of Light, the branches of the Tree of Life reaching toward the kingdom of the Heavenly Father. And see the roots of the Tree of Life descending into the bosom of the Earthly Mother. And the Son of Man is raised to an eternal height and walks in the wonders of the plain; for only the Son of Man carries in his body the roots of the Tree of Life; the same roots that suckle from the bosom of the Earthly Mother; and only the Son of Man carries in his spirit the branches of the Tree of Life; the same branches that reach to the sky, even so to the kingdom of the Heavenly Father.

"And for seven years have you labored throughout the day with the Angels of the Earthly Mother; and for seven years you have slept in the arms of the Heavenly Father. And now your reward shall be great, for it shall be given unto you the gift of tongues, that you may draw to you the full power of your Earthly Mother, and have command over her angels and dominion over all her kingdom; and that you may draw to you the blinding glory of your Heavenly Father, that you may command his angels and enter into life everlasting in the heavenly kingdoms.

"And for seven years these words were not given unto you, for he who uses the gift of tongues to seek after riches, or to hold sway over his enemies, he shall no longer be a Son of Light, but a whelp of the devil and a creature of darkness.

For only the pure water can mirror forth the light of the sun; and that water which has become dank with filth and murk can reflect nothing. And when the body and the spirit of the Son of Man have walked with the Angels of the Earthly Mother and the Heavenly Father for seven years, then is he like the running river under the noonday sun, mirroring forth dazzling lights of brilliant jewels.

"Hear me, Sons of Light, for I will impart to you the gift of tongues, that by speaking to your Earthly Mother in the morning, and to your Heavenly Father in the evening, you may go closer and closer to oneness with the kingdoms of earth and heaven, that oneness for which the Son of Man is destined from the beginning of the times.

"I will make known unto you deep and mysterious things. For I tell you truly, all things exist by God and there is none beside him. Direct your hearts, therefore, that you may walk on the right paths, where his presence is.

"When you open your eyes in the morning, even then before your body has been called by the Angel of Sun, say to yourselves these words, letting them echo in your spirit; for words are like dead leaves when there is no life in them of the spirit. Say, then, these words: 'I enter the eternal and infinite garden of mystery, my spirit in oneness with the Heavenly Father, my body in oneness with the Earthly Mother, my heart in harmony with my Brothers, the Sons of Men, dedicating my spirit, my body, and my heart to the holy, pure and saving Teaching, even that Teaching which of old was known to Enoch.'

"And after these words have entered into your spirit, on the first morning after Sabbath, say these words: 'The Earthly Mother and I are one. Her breath is my breath; her blood is my blood; her bone, her flesh, her bowels, her eyes and ears, are my bone, my flesh, my bowels, my eyes and ears. Never will I desert her, and always will she nourish and sustain my body.' And you will feel the power of the Earthly Mother flowing through your body like the river when it is swollen with rains and courses mightily with a great noise.

"And on the second morning after Sabbath, say these words: 'Angel of Earth, make fruitful my seed, and with your power give life to my body.' Even as your seed creates new life, so courses through the earth the seed of the Angel of Earth: in the grass, in the soil, in all living things that grow from the soil. Know, oh Sons of Light, that the same Angel of Earth that makes your seed into sons also makes the tiny acorn into this mighty oak, and makes the seed-bearing wheat to grow for bread for the Son of Man. And the seed of your body need not enter the body of woman to create life; for the power of the Angel of Earth can create the life of the spirit within, as well as the life of the body without.

"And on the third morning after Sabbath, say these words: 'Angel of Life, enter with strength the limbs of my body.' And with these words embrace the Tree of Life, even as I embrace this brother oak, and you will feel the power of the Angel of Life flow to your arms, and to your legs, and to all the parts of your body, as the sap flows in the tree in the spring, even as it runs out of the trunk, so will the Angel of Life flood your body with the power of the Earthly Mother.

"And on the fourth morning after Sabbath, say these words: 'Angel of joy, descend upon earth, pouring forth beauty and delight to all the children of the Earthly Mother and the Heavenly Father.' And you will go forth into the fields of flowers after rain and give thanks to your Earthly Mother for the sweet odor of blossoms; for I tell you truly, a flower has no other purpose than to bring joy to the heart of the Son of Man. And you will listen with new ears to the song of the birds, and see with new eyes the colors of the sun in its rising and its setting; and all these gifts of the Earthly Mother will cause joy to well forth within you, as a spring wells forth of a sudden in a barren place. And you shall know that no one comes before the Heavenly Father that the Angel of Joy lets not pass; for in joy was the earth created, and in joy did the Earthly Mother and the Heavenly Father give birth to the Son of Man.

"And on the fifth morning after Sabbath, say these words: 'Angel of Sun, enter my body and let me bathe in the fire of life.' And you will feel the rays of the rising sun enter into the center point of your body, there in the center where the Angels of Day and of Night mingle, and the power of the sun shall be yours to direct to any part of your body, for the Angels dwell therein.

"And on the sixth morning after Sabbath, say these words: 'Angel of Water, enter my blood and give the Water of Life to my body.' And you will feel, like the rushing current of the river, the power of the Angel of Water enter your blood, and like the rivulets of a stream, send the power of the Earthly Mother through your blood to all the parts of your body. And it shall be for healing, for the power of the Angel of Water is very great, and when you speak to her, she will send her power wherever you command, for when the Angels of God dwell within the Son of Man, are all things possible.

"And on the seventh morning after Sabbath, say these words: 'Angel of Air, enter with my breath and give the Air of Life to my body.' Know, oh Sons of Light, that the Angel of Air is the messenger of the Heavenly Father, and no one comes before the face of God that the Angel of Air lets not pass. For we do not think of the Angel of Air when we breathe, for we breathe without thought, as the sons of darkness live their lives without thought. But when the power of life enters into your words and into your breathing, then for every time you invoke the Angel of Air, so do you also invoke the unknown Angels of the Heavenly Father; and you will go closer and closer to the heavenly kingdoms.

"And on the Sabbath evening, say these words: 'The Heavenly Father and I are One.' And close your eyes, Sons of Light, and in sleep enter into the unknown realms of the Heavenly Father. And you will bathe in the light of the stars, and the Heavenly Father will hold you in his hand and cause a spring of knowledge to well up within you; a fountain of power, pouring forth living waters, a flood of love and of all-embracing wisdom, like the splendor of Eternal Light. And one day the eyes of your spirit shall open, and you shall know all things.

"And on the first evening after Sabbath, say these words: 'Angel of Eternal Life, descend upon me and give eternal life to my spirit.' And close your eyes, Sons of Light, and in sleep contemplate the oneness of all life everywhere. For I tell you truly, in the daylight hours are our feet on the ground and we have no wings with which to fly. But our spirits are not tied to the earth., and with the coming of night we overcome our attachment to the earth and join with that which is eternal. For the Son of Man is not all that he seems, and only with the eyes of the spirit can we see those golden threads which link us with all life everywhere.

"And on the second evening after Sabbath, say these words: 'Angel of Creative Work, descend upon earth and give abundance to all the Sons of Men.' For this most powerful of the Angels of the Heavenly Father is the cause of movement, and only in movement is life. Work, Sons of Light, in the garden of the Brotherhood to create the kingdom of the heavens upon earth. And as you work, so will the Angel of Creative Work nurture and ripen the seed of your spirit, that you may see God.

"And on the third evening after Sabbath, say these words: 'Peace, peace, peace, Angel of Peace, be always everywhere.' Seek the Angel of Peace in all that lives, in all you do, in every word you speak. For peace is the key to all knowledge, to all mystery, to all life. Where there is no peace, there does Satan reign. And the sons of darkness covet most of all to steal from the Sons of Light their peace. Go, therefore, on this night to the golden stream of light that is the garment of the Angel of Peace. And bring back to the morning the peace of God that surpasses understanding, that with this perfect peace you may comfort the hearts of the Sons of Men.

"And on the fourth evening after Sabbath, say these words: 'Angel of Power, descend on me and fill with power all my deeds.' I tell you truly, just as there is no life on earth without the sun, so there is no life of the spirit without the Angel of Power. What you think and what you feel, these are like the dead scriptures, which are only words on a page, or the dead speech of dead men. But the Sons of Light will not only think, will not only feel, but will also do, and their acts will fulfill their thoughts and feelings, as the golden fruit of summer gives meaning to the green leaves of spring.

'And on the fifth evening after Sabbath, say these words: 'Angel of Love, descend on me and fill with love all my feelings.' For it is by love that the Heavenly Father and the Earthly Mother and the Son of Man become one. Love is eternal. Love is stronger than death. And every night should the Sons of Light bathe in the holy water of the Angel of Love, that with the morning he may baptize the Sons of Men with kind deeds and gentle words. For when the heart of the Son of Light is bathed in love, only kind and gentle words speak forth.

"And on the sixth evening after Sabbath, say these words: 'Angel of Wisdom, descend on me and fill with wisdom all my thoughts.' Know, Sons of Light, that your thoughts are as powerful as the bolt of lightning that stabs through the storm and splits asunder the mighty tree. It was for this that you have waited seven years to learn how to speak with the angels, for you know not the power of your thoughts. Use, then, wisdom in all you think and say and do. For I tell you truly, that which is done without wisdom is as a riderless horse, mouth foaming and eyes wild, running crazed into a yawning chasm. But when the Angel of Wisdom governs your deeds, then is the path to the unknown realms established, and order and harmony govern your lives.

"And these are the communions with the angels which are given to the Sons of Light, that with bodies purified by the Earthly Mother and spirits purified by the Heavenly Father, they may command and serve the angels, continually, from period to period, in the circuits of the day, and in its fixed order; with the coming of light from its source and at the turn of evening and the outgoing of light, at the outgoing of darkness and the coming in of day, continually, in all the generations of time.

"The truth is born out of the spring of Light, falsehood from the well of darkness. The dominion of all the children of truth is in the hands of the Angels of Light so that they may walk in the ways of Light.

"Blessings on all the Sons of Light who have cast their lot with the Law, that walk truthfully in all their ways. May the Law bless you with all good and keep you from all evil, and illumine your hearts with insight into the things of life and grace you with knowledge of things Eternal."

And the crescent moon of peace rose over the mountain and slivers of light shone in the waters of the river. And the Sons of Light as one man knelt in reverence and thanksgiving for the words of Jesus, as he taught them in the ancient ways of their fathers, even as Enoch was taught of old.

And Jesus said: "The Law was planted to reward the Children of Light with healing and abundant peace, with long life, with fruitful seed of everlasting blessings, with eternal joy in immortality of Eternal Light.

"With the coming of day, I embrace my Mother; with the coming of night, I join my Father; and with the outgoing of evening and morning, I will breathe their Law, and I will not interrupt these Communions until the end of time."

THE GIFT OF LIFE IN THE HUMBLE GRASS

It was in the month of Thebet, when the earth was covered with shoots of young grass after the rains, and the covering of emerald green was tender as the fine down of a baby chick. And it was on a bright sun-filled morning that Jesus gathered the new Brothers of the Elect round about him, that they might hear with their ears and understand with their hearts the teachings of their fathers, even as it was taught to Enoch of old.

And Jesus sat beneath a gnarled and ancient tree, holding in his hands a small earthen pot; and in the pot was growing tender grass of wheat, the most perfect among all seedbearing herbs. And the tender grass within the pot was radiant with life, even as the grass and plants which covered the hills far into the distant fields and beyond. And Jesus stroked the grass in the pot with the hands, even as gently as he would touch the head of a little child.

And Jesus said: "Happy are you, Sons of Light, for you have entered into the deathless way and you walk in the path of truth, even as did your fathers of old, who were taught by the Great Ones. With the eyes and ears of the spirit do you see and hear the sights and sounds of the kingdom of the Earthly Mother: the blue sky where dwells the Angel of Air, the foaming river where flows the Angel of Water, the golden light which streams from the Angel of Sun. And I tell you truly, all these are within you as well as without; for your breath, your blood, the fire of life within you, all are one with the Earthly Mother.

But of all these, and more, that most precious gift of your Earthly Mother is the grass beneath your feet, even that grass which you tread upon without thought. Humble and meek is the Angel of Earth, for she has no wings to fly, nor golden rays of light to pierce the mist. But great is her strength and vast is her domain, for she covers the earth with her power, and without her the Sons of Men would be no more, for no man can live without the grass, the trees, and the plants of the Earthly Mother. And these are the gifts of the Angel of Earth to the Sons of Men.

"But now I will speak to you of mysterious things, for I tell you truly, the humble grass is more than food for man and beast. It hides its glory beneath a lowly aspect, as it was told of a ruler of old that he visited the villages of his subjects disguised as a beggar, knowing they would tell many things to such a one, but would fall down in fear before their King. So does the humble grass hide its glory under its coat of humble green, and the Sons of Men walk on it, plough it, feed it to their beasts, but know not what secrets are hidden within it, even those secrets of everlasting life in the heavenly kingdoms.

"But the Sons of Light will know what lies hidden in the grass, for it is given to them to bring comfort to the Sons of Men. Even so are we taught by the Earthly Mother with this -little handful of wheat in a simple pot, even the same earthen pot you use to drink milk and gather the honey of bees. Now the pot is filled with black soil rich with old leaves and moist with the dew of morning, even that most precious gift of the Angel of Earth.

"And I did moisten a handful of wheat, that the Angel of Water entered into it. The Angel of Air did also embrace it, and the Angel of Sun, and the power of the three angels awakened also the Angel of Life within the wheat, and sprout and root were born in each grain.

"Then I put the awakened wheat into the soil of the Angel of Earth, and the power of the Earthly Mother and all her angels entered into the wheat, and when the sun had risen four times the grains had become grass. I tell you truly, there is no greater miracle than this."

And the Brothers looked with reverence at the tender blades of grass in the hands of Jesus, and one asked him: "Master, what is the secret of the grass you hold in your hands? Why is it different from that grass that covers the hills and the mountains?"

And Jesus answered "It is not different, Son of Light. All grass, all trees, all plants, in every part of the world, all are part of the kingdom of the Earthly Mother. But I have separated in this pot a small portion of your Mother's kingdom, that you may touch her with the hands of the spirit, and that her power may enter into your body.

"For I tell you truly, there is a Holy Stream of Life which gave birth to the Earthly Mother and all her angels. Invisible is this Stream of Life to the eyes of the Sons of Men, for they walk in darkness and see not the Angels of the Day and of the Night that surround them and hover over them. But the Sons of Light have walked for seven years with the Angels of the Day and of the Night, and now they are given the secrets of communion with the angels. And the eyes of your spirit shall be opened, and you will see and hear and touch the Stream of Life that gave birth to the Earthly Mother. And you will enter the Holy Stream of Life, and it will carry you with infinite tenderness to everlasting life in the kingdom of your Heavenly Father."

"How shall we do this, Master?" some asked in amazement. "What secrets must we know to see and hear and touch this Holy Stream of Life?".

And Jesus did not answer. But he placed his two hands around the growing blades of grass in the pot, gently, as if it were the forehead of a little child. And he closed his eyes, and around him were waves of light, shimmering in the sun, as the summer heat makes the light to tremble under a cloudless sky. And the Brothers knelt and bowed their heads in reverence before the power of the angels which poured forth from the sitting figure of Jesus; and still he sat in silence, with his hands closed as if in prayer around the blades of grass.

And no one knew if an hour had passed, or a year, for time stood still and it was as if all creation held its breath. And Jesus opened his eyes, and the scent of blossoms filled the air as Jesus spoke: "Here is the secret, Sons of Light; here in the humble grass. Here is the meeting place of the Earthly Mother and the Heavenly Father; here is the Stream of Life which gave birth to all creation; I tell you truly, only to the Son of Man is it given to see and hear and touch the Stream of Life which flows between the Earthly and Heavenly Kingdoms. Place your hands around the tender grass of the Angel of Earth, and you will see and hear and touch the power of all the angels."

And one by one, each of the Brothers sat in reverence before the power of the angels, holding in his hands the tender grass. And each one felt the Stream of Life enter his body with the force of a rushing stream after a spring storm. And the power of the angels flowed into their hands, up into their arms, and shook them mightily, even as the wind of the north shakes the branches of trees. And all of them wondered at the power in the humble grass, that it could contain all the angels, and the kingdoms of the Earthly Mother and the heavenly Father. And they sat before Jesus and were taught by him.

And Jesus said: "Behold, Sons of Light, the lowly grass. See wherein are contained all the Angels of the Earthly Mother and the Heavenly Father. For now have you stepped into the Stream of Life, and its currents will carry you in time to everlasting life in the kingdom of your Heavenly Father.

"For in the grass are all the angels. Here is the Angel of Sun, here in the brightness of the green color of the blades of wheat. For no one can look upon the sun when it is high in the heavens, for the eyes of the Son of Man are blinded by its radiant light. And it is for this that the Angel of Sun turns to green all that to which she gives life, that the Son of Man may look upon the many and various shades of green and find strength and comfort therein. I tell you truly, all that is green and with life has the power of the Angel of Sun within it, even these tender blades of young wheat.

"And so does the Angel of Water bless the grass, for I tell you truly, there is more of the Angel of Water within the grass than any of the other Angels of the Earthly Mother. For if you crush within your hands the grass, you will feel the water of life, which is the blood of the Earthly Mother. And all through the days when you touch the grass and enter into the Stream of Life, do you give to the soil a few drops of water, that the grass may be renewed by the power of the Angel of Water.

"Know, also, that the Angel of Air is within the grass, for all that is living and green is the home of the Angel of Air. Put your face close to the grass, breathe deeply, and let the Angel of Air enter deep within your body. For she abides in the grass, as the oak abides in the acorn, and as the fish abides in the sea.

"The Angel of Earth is she who gives birth to the grass, even as the babe in the womb lives from the nourishment of his mother, so does the earth give of itself to the grain of wheat, causing it to shoot forth to embrace the Angel of Air. I tell you truly, each grain of wheat that bursts forth upward to the sky is a victory over death, where Satan reigns. For Life always begins again.

"It is the Angel of Life that flows through the blades of grass into the body of the Son of Light, shaking him with her power. For the grass is Life and the Son of Light is Life, and Life flows between the Son of Light and the blades of grass, making a bridge to the Holy Stream of Light which gave birth to all creation.

"And when the Son of Light holds between his hands the blades of grass, it is the Angel of Joy which fills his body with music. To enter into the Stream of Life is to be one with the song of the bird, the colors of the wild flowers, the scent of the sheaves of grain, newly turned over in the fields. I tell you truly, when the Son of Man feels not joy in his heart, he labors for Satan and brings hope to the sons of darkness. There is no sadness in the kingdom of Light, only the Angel of Joy. Learn, then, from the tender blades of grass the song of the Angel of Joy, that the Sons of Light may walk with her always and so comfort the hearts of the Sons of Men.

"The Earthly Mother is she who provides for our bodies, for we are born of her, and have our life in her. So does she provide for us food in the very blades of grass we touch with our hands. For I tell you truly, it is not only as bread that wheat may nourish us. We may eat also of the tender blades of grass, that the strength of the Earthly Mother may enter into us. But chew well the blades, for the Son of Man has teeth unlike those of the beasts, and only when we chew well the blades of grass can the Angel of Water enter our blood and give us strength. Eat, then, Sons of Light, of this most perfect herb from the table of our Earthly Mother, that your days may be long upon the earth, for such finds favor in the eyes of God.

"I tell you truly, the Angel of Power enters into you when you touch the Stream of Life through the blades of grass. For the Angel of Power is as a shining light that surrounds every living thing, just as the full moon is encircled by rings of radiance, and as the mist rises up from the fields when the sun climbs in the sky. And the Angel of Power enters into the Son of Light when his heart is pure and his desire is only to comfort and teach the Sons of Men. Touch, then, the blades of grass, and feel the Angel of Power enter the tips of your fingers, flow upwards through your body, and shake you till you tremble with wonder and awe.

"Know, also, that the Angel of Love is present in the blades of grass, for love is in the giving, and great is the love given to the Sons of Light by the tender blades of grass. For I tell you truly, the Stream of Life runs through every living thing, and all that lives, bathes in the Holy Stream of Life. And when the Son of Light touches with love the blades of grass, so do the blades of grass return his love, and lead him to the Stream of Life where he may find life everlasting. And this love never exhausts itself, for its source is in the Stream of Life which flows into the Eternal Sea, and no matter how far does the Son of Man stray from his Earthly Mother and his Heavenly Father, the touch of the blades of grass will always bring a message from the Angel of Love; and his feet shall bathe again in the Holy Stream of Life.

"Lo, it is the Angel of Wisdom that governs the movement of the planets, the circle of the seasons, and the orderly growth of all living things. So does the Angel of Wisdom ordain the communion of the Sons of Light with the Stream of Life, through the tender blades of grass. For I tell you truly, your body is holy, because it bathes in the Stream of Life, which is Eternal Order.

"Touch the blades of grass, Sons of Light, and touch the Angel of Eternal Life. For if you look with the eyes of the spirit, you will truly see that the grass is eternal. Now it is young and tender, with the brightness of the newborn babe. Soon it will be tall and gracious, as the sapling tree with its first fruits. Then it will yellow with age, and bow its head in patience, as lies the field after the harvest. Finally, it will wither, for the small earthen pot cannot contain the full lifespan of the wheat. But it does not die, for the brown leaves return to the Angel of Earth, and she holds the plant in her arms and bids it sleep, and all the angels work within the faded leaves and lo, they are changed and do not die but rise again in another guise. And so do the Sons of Light never see death, but find themselves changed and risen to everlasting Life.

"And so does the Angel of Work never sleep, but sends the roots of the wheat deep into the Angel of Earth, that the shoots of tender green may overcome death and the reign of Satan. For life is movement, and the Angel of Work is never still, even does he labor without ceasing in the vineyard of the Lord. Close your eyes when you touch the grass, Sons of Light, but fall not asleep, for to touch the Stream of Life is to touch the eternal rhythm of the everlasting kingdoms, and to bathe in the Stream of Life is to feel more and more the power of the Angel of Work within you, creating on earth the Kingdom of Heaven.

"Peace is the gift of the Stream of Life to the Sons of Light. Wherefore do we always greet each other, 'Peace be with you.' Even so does the grass greet your body with the kiss of Peace. I tell you truly, Peace is not just the absence of war, for very quickly can the peaceful river turn into a raging torrent, and the same waves that lull the boat can quickly break it to pieces against the rocks. So does violence lie in wait for the Sons of Man, when they keep not the vigil of Peace. Touch the blades of grass, and thereby touch the Stream of Life. Therein you will find Peace, the Peace built with the power of all the angels. Even so with that Peace will the rays of Holy Light cast out all darkness.

"When the Sons of Light are one with the Stream of Life, then will the power of the blades of grass guide them to the everlasting kingdom of the Heavenly Father. And you shall know more of those mysteries which is not yet time for you to hear. For there are other Holy Streams in the everlasting kingdoms; I tell you truly, the heavenly kingdoms are crossed and crossed again by streams of golden light, arching far beyond the dome of the sky and having no end. And the Sons of Light shall travel by these streams forever, knowing not death, guided by the eternal love of the Heavenly Father. And I tell you truly, all these mysteries are contained in the humble grass, when you touch it with tenderness and open your heart to the Angel of Life within.

"Gather, then, the grains of wheat and plant them in small earthen pots; and every day with glad heart commune with the angels, that they may guide you to the Holy Stream of Life, and you may bring back from its eternal source comfort and strength for the Sons of Men. For I tell you truly, all that you learn, all that your eyes of the spirit see, all that your cars of the spirit hear, all this is as a hollow reed in the wind if you do not send forth a message of truth and light to the Sons of Men. For by the fruit do we know the worth of the tree. And to love is to teach without end, without ceasing. For so were your fathers taught of old, even our Father Enoch. Go now, and peace be with you."

And Jesus held forth the little pot with the blades of young grass, as if in blessing, and walked toward the sun-filled hills, along the shore of the river, as was the custom of all the Brothers. And the others followed, each holding to him the words of Jesus, as it were a precious jewel within his breast.

THE SEVENFOLD PEACE

"Peace be with you," spoke the Elder in greeting to the Brothers who had gathered for the teachings

"Peace be with you," they answered; and they walked together along the bank of the river, for so was their custom when an Elder taught the Brothers, that they might share the teachings with the Angels of the Earthly Mother: of air, of sun, of water, of earth, of life, and of joy.

And the Elder said to the Brothers: "I would speak to you of peace, for of all the Angels of the Heavenly Father, peace is that for which the world most yearns, as a tired babe longs to put his head on his mother's breast. It is the lack of peace that troubles the kingdoms, even when they are not at war. For violence and warfare may reign in a kingdom even when the sounds of clashing swords are not heard. Though no armies march one against the other, still there is no peace when the Sons of Men walk not with the Angels of God. I tell you truly, many are those who do not know peace; for they are at war with their own body; they are at war with their thoughts; they have no peace with their fathers, their mothers, their children; they have no peace with their friends and neighbors; they know not the beauty of the Holy Scrolls; they labor not through the day in the kingdom of their Earthly Mother; nor do they sleep at night in the arms of their Heavenly Father. Peace reigns not within them, forever do they thirst for that which in the end brings only misery and pain, even those trappings of riches and fame which Satan uses to tempt the Sons of Men; and they live in ignorance of the Law, even that Holy Law by which we live: the path of the Angels of the Earthly Mother and the Heavenly Father."

"How, then, may we bring peace to our brothers, Master?" asked some of the Elder, "for we would that all the Sons of Men share in the blessings of the Angel of Peace."

And he answered: "Truly, only he who is at peace with all the Angels can shed the light of peace on others. Therefore, first be at peace with all the Angels of the Earthly Mother and the Heavenly Father. For the winds of a storm stir and trouble the waters of the river, and only the stillness that follows can calm them once again. Take care when your brother asks you for bread, that you give him not stones. Live first in peace with all the angels, for then your peace will be as a fountain that does replenish itself with the giving, and the more you give, so the more you will be given, for such is the Law.

"Three are the dwellings of the Son of Man, and no one may come before the face of God who knows not the Angel of Peace in each of the three. These are his body, his thoughts, and his feelings. When the Angel of Wisdom guides his thoughts, when the Angel of Love purifies his feelings, and when the deeds of his body reflect both love and wisdom, then does the Angel of Peace guide him unfailingly to the throne of his Heavenly Father. And he should pray without ceasing that the power of Satan, with all his diseases and uncleannesses, may be cast out of all of his three dwellings; that Power and Wisdom and Love may reign in his body, his thoughts, and his feelings.

"First shall the Son of Man seek peace with his own body; for his body is as a mountain pond that reflects the sun when it is still and clear; but when it is full of mud and stones, it reflects nothing. First must Satan be cast out of the body, that the Angels of God may enter again and dwell therein. Truly, no peace can reign in the body unless it is as a temple of the Holy Law. Therefore, when he who suffers with pains and grievous plagues asks for your help, tell him to renew himself with fasting and with prayer. Tell him to invoke the Angel of Sun, the Angel of Water, and the Angel of Air, that they may enter his body and cast out of it the power of Satan. Show him the baptism within, and the baptism without. Tell him always to eat of the table of our Earthly Mother, spread with her gifts: the fruits of the trees, the grasses of the fields, the milk of beasts good for eating, and the honey of bees. He shall not invoke the power of Satan by eating the flesh of beasts, for he who kills, kills his brother, and whoso eats the flesh of slain beasts, eats the body of death. Tell him to prepare his food with the fire of life, not the fire of death, for the living Angels of the living God serve only living men.

"And though he sees them not, and hears them not, and touches them not, still is he every moment surrounded by the power of God's angels. While his eyes and ears are closed by ignorance of the Law and thirst for the pleasures of Satan, he will not see them, nor hear them, nor touch them. But when he fasts and prays to the living God to cast out all the diseases and uncleannesses of Satan, then will his eyes and ears be opened, and he will find peace.

"For not only he suffers who harbors the diseases of Satan within him, but his mother, his father, his wife, his children, his companions, these suffer also, for no man is an island unto himself, and the powers that flow through him, whether they be of the angels or of Satan, truly these powers do unto others for good or for evil.

"After this manner, therefore, pray to your Heavenly Father, when the sun is high at midday: 'Our Father who art in heaven, send to all the Sons of Men your Angel of Peace; and send to our body the Angel of Life to dwell therein forever.'

"Then shall the Son of Man seek peace with his own thoughts; that the Angel of Wisdom may guide him. For I tell you truly, there is no greater power in heaven and earth than the thoughts of the Son of Man. Though unseen by the eyes of the body, yet each thought has mighty strength, even such strength as can shake the heavens.

"For to no other creature in the kingdom of the Earthly Mother is it given the power of thought, for all beasts that crawl and birds that fly, live not of their own thinking but of the one Law that governs all. Only to the Sons of Men is it given the power of thought, even that thought that can break the bonds of death. Do not think because it cannot be seen, that thought has no power. I tell you truly, the lightning that cleaves the mighty oak, or the quaking that opens up cracks in the earth, these are as the play of children compared with the power of thought. Truly each thought of darkness, whether it be of malice, or anger, or vengeance, these wreak destruction like that of fire sweeping through dry kindling under a windless sky. But man does not see the carnage, nor does he hear the piteous cries of his victims, for he is blind to the world of the spirit.

"But when this power is guided by holy Wisdom, then the thoughts of the Son of Man lead him to the heavenly kingdoms and thus is paradise built on earth; then it is that your thoughts uplift the souls of men, as the cold waters of a rushing stream revive your body in the summer heat.

"When first a fledgling bird tries to fly, his wings cannot support him, and he falls again and again to earth. But he tries again and one day he soars aloft, leaving earth and his nest far behind. So is it with the thoughts of the Sons of Men. The longer he walks with the angels and keeps their Law, so do the stronger his thoughts become in holy Wisdom. And I tell you truly, that day will come when his thoughts will overcome even the kingdom of death and soar to everlasting life in the heavenly kingdoms; for with their thoughts guided by holy Wisdom do the Sons of Men build a bridge of light thereby to reach God.

"After this manner, therefore, pray to your Heavenly Father, when the sun is high at midday: 'Our Father who art in heaven, send to all the Sons of Men your Angel of Peace; and send to our thoughts the Angel of Power, that we may break the bonds of death.

"Then shall the Son of Man seek peace with his own feelings; that his family may delight in his loving kindness, even his father, his mother, his wife, his children, and his children's children. For the Heavenly Father is a hundred times greater than all fathers by seed and by blood, and the Earthly Mother is a hundred times greater than all mothers by the body, and your true brothers are all those who do the will of your Heavenly Father and of your Earthly Mother, and not your brothers by blood. Even so, shall you see the Heavenly Father in your father by seed, and your Earthly Mother in your mother by the body, for are not these also children of the Heavenly Father and the Earthly Mother? Even so shall you love your brothers by blood as you love all your true brothers who walk with the angels, for are not these also children of the Heavenly Father and the Earthly Mother? I tell you truly, it is easier to love those newly met, than those of our own house, who have known our weaknesses, and heard our words of anger, and seen us in our nakedness, for they know us as we know ourselves, and we are ashamed. Then shall we call on the Angel of Love to enter into our feelings, that they be purifiers And all that was before impatience and discord, will turn to harmony and peace, as the parched ground drinks in the gentle rain and becomes green and soft, tender with new life.

"For many and grievous are the sufferings of the Sons of Men when they cleave not to the Angel of Love. Truly, a man without love casts a dark shadow on everyone he meets, most of all those with whom he lives; his harsh and angry words fall on his brothers like fetid air rising from a stagnant pool. And he suffers most who speaks them, for the darkness that encloses him invites Satan and his devils.

"But when he calls on the Angel of Love, then is the darkness dispersed, and the light of sunshine streams from him, and the colors of the rainbow swirl about his head, and gentle rain falls from his fingers, and he brings peace and strength to all those who draw near to him.

"After this manner, therefore, pray to your Heavenly Father, when the sun is high at midday: 'Our Father who art in heaven, send to all the Sons of Men your Angel of Peace; and send to those of our seed and of our blood the Angel of Love, that peace and harmony may dwell in our house forever.'

"Then shall the Son of Man seek peace with other Sons of Men, even with the Pharisees and priests, even with beggars and the homeless, even with kings and governors. For all are Sons of Men, whatever be their station, whatever be their calling, whether their eyes have been opened to see the heavenly kingdoms, or whether they yet walk in darkness and ignorance.

"For the justice of men may reward the undeserving and punish the innocent, but Holy Law is the same for all, whether beggar or king, whether shepherd or priest.

"Seek peace with all the Sons of Men, and let it be known of the Brothers of Light, that we have lived according to the Holy Law since the time of Enoch of old, and before. For we are not rich, neither are we poor. And we do share all things, even our garments and the tools we use to till the soil. And together we work in the fields with all the angels, bringing forth the gifts of the Earthly Mother for all to eat.

"For the strongest of the Angels of the Heavenly Father, the Angel of Work, blesses each man who works in the way best for him, for then shall he know neither want nor excess. Truly is there abundance for all men in the kingdoms of the Earthly Mother and the Heavenly Father when each man works at his task; for when a man shirks his task, then another must take it up, for we are given all things in the kingdoms of heaven and earth at the price of labor.

"Always have the Brothers of Light lived where rejoice the Angels of the Earthly Mother: near rivers, near trees, near flowers, near the music of birds; where sun and rain may embrace the body, which is the temple of the spirit. Nor do we have ought to do with the edicts of rulers; neither do we uphold them, as our law is the Law of the Heavenly Father and the Earthly Mother; neither do we oppose them, for no one rules save by the will of God. Rather do we strive to live according to the Holy Law and strengthen always that which is good in all things; then will the kingdom of darkness be changed to the kingdom of light; for where there is light, how then can darkness remain?

"After this manner, therefore, pray to your Heavenly Father, when the sun is high at midday: 'Our Father who art in heaven, send to all the Sons of Men your Angel of Peace; and send to all humankind the Angel of Work, that having a holy task we should not ask for any other blessing.'

"Then shall the Son of Man seek peace with the knowledge of the ages past; for I tell you truly, in the Holy Scrolls is a treasure a hundred times greater than any of jewels and gold in the richest of kingdoms, and more precious, for surely they contain all the wisdom revealed by God to the Sons of Light, even those traditions which came to us through Enoch of old, and before him on an endless path into the past, the teachings of the Great Ones. And these are our inheritance, even as the son inherits all the possessions of his father when he shows himself to be worthy of his father's blessing. Truly, by studying the teachings of ageless wisdom do we come to know God, for I tell you truly, the Great Ones saw God face to face; even so, when we read the Holy Scrolls do we touch the feet of God.

"And when once we see with the eyes of wisdom and hear with the cars of understanding the ageless truths of the Holy Scrolls, then must we go among the Sons of Men and teach them, for if we jealously hide the holy knowledge, pretending that it belongs only to us, then we are as one who finds a spring high in the mountains, and rather than let it flow into the valley to quench the thirst of man and beast, buries it under rocks and dirt, thereby robbing himself of water, as well. Go among the Sons of Men and tell them of the Holy Law, that they may thereby save themselves and enter the heavenly kingdoms. But tell them in words they may understand, in parables from nature that speak to the heart, for the deed must first live as desire in the awakened heart.

"After this manner, therefore, pray to your Heavenly Father, when the sun is high at midday: 'Our Father who art in heaven, send to all the Sons of Men your Angel of Peace; and send to our knowledge the Angel of Wisdom, that we may walk in the paths of the Great Ones who have seen the face of God.

"Then shall the Son of Man seek peace with the kingdom of his Earthly Mother, for none can live long, neither be happy, but he who honors his Earthly Mother and does her laws. For your breath is her breath; your blood her blood; your bone her bone; your flesh her flesh; your bowels her bowels; your eyes and your ears are her eyes and her ears.

"I tell you truly, you are one with the Earthly Mother; she is in you, and you in her. Of her were you born, in her do you live, and to her shall you return again. It is the blood of our Earthly Mother which falls from the clouds and flows in the rivers; it is the breath of our Earthly Mother which, whispers in the leaves of the forest and blows with a mighty wind from the mountains; sweet and firm is the flesh of our Earthly Mother in the fruits of the trees; strong and unflinching are the bones of our Earthly Mother in the giant rocks and stones which stand as sentinels of the lost times; truly, we are one with our Earthly Mother, and he who clings to the laws of his Mother, to him shall his Mother cling also.

"But there will come a day when the Son of Man will turn his face from his Earthly Mother and betray her, even denying his Mother and his birthright. Then shall he sell her into slavery, and her flesh shall be ravaged, her blood polluted, and her breath smothered; he will bring the fire of death into all the parts of her kingdom, and his hunger will devour all her gifts and leave in their place only a desert.

"All these things will he do out of ignorance of the Law, and as a man dying slowly cannot smell his own stench, so will the Son of Man be blind to the truth: that as he plunders and ravages and destroys his Earthly Mother, so does he plunder and ravage and destroy himself. For he was born of his Earthly Mother, and he is one with her, and all that he does to his Mother even so does he do to himself.

"Long ago, before the Great Flood, the Great Ones walked the earth, and the giant trees, even those which now are no more than legend, were their home and their kingdom. They lived many score of generations, for they ate from the table of the Earthly Mother, and slept in the arms of the Heavenly Father, and they knew not disease, old age, nor death. To the Sons of Men did they bequeath all the glory of their kingdoms, even the hidden knowledge of the Tree of Life which stands in the middle of the Eternal Sea. But the eyes of the Sons of Men were blinded by the visions of Satan, and by promises of power, even that power which conquers by might and by blood. And then did the Son of Man sever the golden threads that bound him to his Earthly Mother and his Heavenly Father; he stepped from the Holy Stream of Life where his body, his thoughts, and his feelings were one with the Law, and began to use only his own thoughts, his own feelings, and his own deeds, making hundreds of laws, where before there was only One.

"And so did the Sons of Men exile themselves from their home, and ever since have they huddled behind their stone walls, hearing not the sighing of the wind in the tall trees of the forests beyond their towns.

"I tell you truly, the Book of Nature is a Holy Scroll, and if you would have the Sons of Men save themselves and find everlasting life, teach them how once again to read from the living pages of the Earthly Mother. For in everything that is life is the Law written. It is written in the grass, in the trees, in rivers, mountains, birds of the sky and fishes of the sea; and most of all within the Son of Man. Only when he returns to the bosom of his Earthly Mother will he find everlasting life and the Stream of Life which leads to his Heavenly Father; only then may the dark vision of the future come not to pass.

"After this manner, therefore, pray to your Heavenly Father, when the sun is high at midday: 'Our Father who art in heaven, send to all the Sons of Men your Angel of Peace; and send to the kingdom of our Earthly Mother the Angel of joy, that our hearts may be full of singing and gladness as we nestle in the arms of our Mother.

At last, shall the Son of Man seek peace with the kingdom of his Heavenly Father; for truly, the Son of Man is only born of his father by seed and of his mother by the body, that he may find his true inheritance and know at last that he is the Son of the King.

"The Heavenly Father is the One Law, who fashioned the stars, the sun, the light and the darkness, and the Holy Law within our souls. Everywhere is he, and there is nowhere he is not. All in our understanding, and all we know not, all is governed by the Law. The falling of leaves, the flow of rivers, the music of insects at night, all these are ruled by the Law.

"In our Heavenly Father's realm there are many mansions, and many are the hidden things you cannot know of yet. I tell you truly, the kingdom of our Heavenly Father is vast, so vast that no man can know its limits, for there are none. Yet the whole of his kingdom may be found in the smallest drop of dew on a wild flower, or in the scent of newly-cut grass in the fields under the summer sun. Truly, there are no words to describe the kingdom of the Heavenly Father.

"Glorious, indeed, is the inheritance of the Son of Man, for to him only is it given to enter the Stream of Life which leads him to the kingdom of his Heavenly Father. But first he must seek and find peace with his body, with his thoughts, with his feelings, with the Sons of Men, with holy knowledge, and with the kingdom of the Earthly Mother. For I tell you truly, this is the vessel which will carry the Son of Man on the Stream of Life to his Heavenly Father. He must have peace that is sevenfold before he can know the one peace which surpasses understanding, even that of his Heavenly Father.

"After this manner, therefore, pray to your Heavenly Father, when the sun is high at midday: 'Our Father who art in heaven, send to all the Sons of Men your Angel of Peace; and send to your kingdom, our Heavenly Father, your Angel of Eternal Life, that we may soar beyond the stars and live forever.'"

And then the Elder was quiet, and a great stillness stole over the Brothers, and no one wished to speak. The shadows of late afternoon played on the river, still and silvery as glass, and in the darkening sky could faintly be seen the filigree crescent moon of peace. And the great peace of the Heavenly Father wrapt them all in deathless love.

THE HOLY STREAMS

Into the innermost circle have you come, into the Mystery of Mysteries, that which was old when our Father Enoch was young and walked the earth. Around and around have you come on your journey of many years, always following the path of righteousness, living according to the Holy Law and the sacred vows of our Brotherhood, and you have made of your body a holy temple wherein dwell the Angels of God. Many years have you shared the daylight hours with the Angels of the Earthly Mother; many years have you slept in the arms of the Heavenly Father, taught by his unknown angels. You have learned that the laws of the Son of Man are seven, of the angels three, and of God, one. Now you shall know of the three laws of the angels, the mystery of the three Holy Streams, and the ancient way to traverse them; so shall you bathe in the light of heaven and at last behold the revelation of the Mystery of Mysteries: the Law of God, which is One.

Now in the hour before the rising of the sun, just before the Angels of the Earthly Mother breathe life into the still-sleeping earth, then do you enter into the Holy Stream of Life. It is your Brother Tree who holds the mystery of this Holy Stream, and it is your Brother Tree that you will embrace in your thought, even as by day you embrace him in greeting when you walk along the lakeshore. And you shall be one with the tree, for in the beginning of the times so did we all share in the Holy Stream of Life that gave birth to all creation. And as you embrace your Brother Tree, the power of the Holy Stream of Life will fill your whole body, and you will tremble before its might. Then breathe deeply of the Angel of Air, and say the word "Life" with the outgiving of breath. Then you will become in truth the Tree of Life which sinks its roots deep into the Holy Stream of Life from an eternal source. And as the Angel of Sun warms the earth, and all the creatures of land and water and air rejoice in the new day, so will your body and spirit rejoice in the Holy Stream of life that flows to you through your Brother Tree.

And when the sun is high in the heavens, then shall you seek the Holy Stream of Sound. In the heat of noontide, all creatures are still and seek the shade; the Angels of the Earthly Mother are silent for a space. Then it is that you shall let into your ears the Holy Stream of Sound; for it can only be heard in the silence. Think on the streams that are born in the desert after a sudden storm, and the roaring sound of the waters as they rush past. Truly, this is the voice of God, if you did but know it. For as it is written, in the beginning was the Sound, and the Sound was with God, and the Sound was God. I tell you truly, when we are born, we enter the world with the sound of God in our ears, even the singing of the vast chorus of the sky, and the holy chant of the stars in their fixed rounds; it is the Holy Stream of Sound that traverses the vault of stars and crosses the endless kingdom of the Heavenly Father. It is ever in our ears, so do we hear it not. Listen for it, then, in the silence of noontide; bathe in it, and let the rhythm of the music of God beat in your ears until you are one with the Holy Stream of Sound. It was this Sound which formed the earth and the world, and brought forth the mountains, and set the stars in their thrones of glory in the highest heavens.

And you shall bathe in the Stream of Sound, and the music of its waters shall flow over you; for in the beginning of the times so did we all share in the Holy Stream of Sound that gave birth to all creation. And the mighty roaring of the Stream of Sound will fill your whole body, and you will tremble before its might. Then breathe deeply of the Angel of Air, and become the sound itself, that the Holy Stream of Sound may carry you to the endless kingdom of the Heavenly Father, there where the rhythm of the world rises and falls.

And when darkness gently closes the eyes of the Angels of the Earthly Mother, then shall you also sleep, that your spirit may join the unknown Angels of the Heavenly Father. And in the moments before you sleep, then shall you think of the bright and glorious stars, the white, shining, far-seen and far-piercing stars. For your thoughts before sleep are as the bow of the skillful archer, that sends the arrow where he wills. Let your thoughts before sleep be with the stars; for the stars are Light, and the Heavenly Father is Light, even that Light which is a thousand times brighter than the brightness of a thousand suns. Enter the Holy Stream of Light, that the shackles of death may loose their hold forever, and breaking free from the bonds of earth, ascend the Holy Stream of Light through the blazing radiance of the stars, into the endless kingdom of the Heavenly Father.

Unfold your wings of light, and in the eye of your thought, soar with the stars into the farthest reaches of heaven, where untold suns blaze with light. For at the beginning of the times, the Holy Law said, let there be Light, and there was Light. And you shall be one with it, and the power of the Holy Light Stream will fill your whole body, and you will tremble before its might. Say the word "Light," as you breathe deeply of the Angel of Air, and you will become the Light itself; and the Holy Stream will carry you to the endless kingdom of the Heavenly Father, there losing itself in the eternal Sea of Light which gives birth to all creation. And you shall be one with the Holy Stream of Light, always before you sleep in the arms of the Heavenly Father.

I tell you truly, your body was made not only to breathe, and eat, and think, but it was also made to enter the Holy Stream of Life. And your ears were made not only to hear the words of men, the song of birds, and the music of falling rain, but they were also made to hear the Holy Stream of Sound. And your eyes were made not only to see the rising and setting of the sun, the ripple of sheaves of grain, and the words of the Holy Scrolls, but they were also made to see the Holy Stream of Light. One day your body will return to the Earthly Mother; even also your ears and your eyes. But the Holy Stream of Life, the Holy Stream of Sound, and the Holy Stream of Light, these were never born, and can never die. Enter the Holy Streams, even that Life, that Sound, and that Light which gave you birth; that you may reach the kingdom of the Heavenly Father and become one with him, even as the river empties into the far-distant sea.

More than this cannot be told, for the Holy Streams will take you to that place where words are no more, and even the Holy Scrolls cannot record the mysteries therein.

www.ingramcontent.com/pod-product-compliance
Lightning Source LLC
Chambersburg PA
CBHW030230170426
43201CB00006B/172